Out of Place

Homelessness in America

Richard Sweeney

Modesto Junior College

 HarperCollins*College*Publishers

Acquisitions Editor: Alan McClare
Cover Design: Heather A. Ziegler
Production Administrator: Linda Greenberg
Printer and Binder: R. R. Donnelley & Sons Company
Cover Printer: Phoenix Color Corp.

Out of Place: Homelessness in America

Library of Congress Cataloging-in-Publication Data

Sweeney, Richard.
    Out of place : homelessness in America / Richard Sweeney.
        p.   cm.
    Includes bibliographical references.
    ISBN 0-06-501639-4
    1. Homeless persons--United States. 2. Homelessness--Government
policy--United States. 3. Shelters for the homeless--United States-
-Case studies.   I. Title.
HV4505.S94   1993
362.5'0973--dc20   93-10132
                                                    CIP

Photo Credits
page 34:   Richard Sweeney
page 85:   Laffont, Sygma
page 92:   Richard Sweeney
page 99:   UPI/Bettmann

93 94 95 96 9 8 7 6 5 4 3 2 1

To Lillian

Contents

Preface

Near the entrance to San Francisco's Chinatown a man in his thirties is huddled against a brick building. He is disheveled, crying, alone, and clearly out of place in a city of such great wealth. He rests his right hand on a foot that is bloody and swollen. And then a stranger, a woman, generously places a small sack of food alongside the man, and quietly leaves.

> For these are scenes that grip the heart, an' when yer tears are dried,
> Ye find the home is dearer than it was, an' sanctified;
>
> (Guest, p.261)

These scenes that we often encounter on the streets are the most visible aspects of homelessness for most of us. But what homelessness is mainly about is invisible to us. We are not likely to see the work of various charities, programs, or bureaucracies that attempt to deal with homelessness. We are not able to actually see such social processes as deinstitutionalization or deindustrialization. And we are not likely to know what ever happens to these people that, for a moment, appear in our lives.

As generous as people may be, homelessness

cannot be solved by individual acts of compassion. It requires a comprehensive approach that only governments can manage. Until recently, our efforts to solve the problems of homelessness have been minimal, and today, we have a problem like that of no other modern nation. Why is it that such a wealthy country allows such a miserable condition to remain? *Out of Place: Homelessness in America* attempts to bring together those complex reasons and the findings and recommendations from experts in the field.

I would like to thank the following people for their help in the publication of this book. My editor, Alan McClare has, as always, consistently offered encouragement and professional advice that is appreciated and respected. I also wish to thank Richard Appelbaum of U.C. Santa Barbara for taking the time from his busy schedule to offer comments and criticisms that reflect his standing as an expert in the field. And finally, I wish to express thanks to Jennie, my wife and companion, who always manages to be there in mind and spirit.

Richard Sweeney
January 1993

Out of Place

Chapter One
Introduction

Among the many aromas that greet the residents inside the overheated shelter on the west side of New York City is the unmistakable scent of chlorine bleach. It has permeated the hot air and settled around the several hundred people that have recently wakened. Windows with waves in the glass direct the midmorning light onto many of the beds in the dormitory-style room. Frank, a thirty-four-year-old former warehouseman with an "anxiety and nervousness problem," is fearful of being attacked during the night. He sleeps on his side because otherwise, he says, "I'd be a flat target." John T., who has been homeless for most of the last fifteen years, normally stays in the shelter, which he calls "warriorland," where he can get his "three hots and a cot." He would like to be able to live in a more permanent and private place, but he is not yet willing to give up the use of crack cocaine.

In Los Angeles, the lone resident of an infrequently visited freeway cavern is awakened earlier than usual. Billy, who was recently released from a mental institution, has seen his thirty-year life take many more turns for the worse than for the better. His aches and pains and disturbing thoughts are daily annoyances that are not normally diagnosed, except for perhaps later today after a long wait at a public clinic.

Not far away, near the unfinished part of a new freeway, residents of a "tent city" are beginning their morning routine, if any routine is possible after being in existence for only several days. Lionel and Veralina take turns dressing their small son while helping to coordinate the morning activities. "We're not real leaders - official or anything, y'know," says Lionel, explaining that this is part of an emergency shelter protest. "The police have been told not to do anything against us for now until they figure out the legality stuff." Both have worked intermittently since they were married, but not enough to prevent them from drifting into homelessness for the first time in their young lives. The camp residents, some of whom are also young families with jobs and small children, are prepared to rise early and pack their few belongings at a moment's notice. A local business, sympathetic to the protest, had arranged for a portable toilet to be delivered, but it has not yet arrived.

In Houston, Rosa, a forty-two-year-old homeless woman, considers her options. To arrive early to get in line for the free 10:30 meal at the soup kitchen means only an hour or so wait. On the other hand, arriving close to noon will result in no wait at all, but it means going without food for an additional hour and a half. Either way, the better part of the morning might be spent checking optimistically for new events in the homeless world. The Welfare Office, the Clinic, the drop-in center, or other places, usually located an uncomfortable distance from each other, may be visited if it can be worked out. Much depends upon the unknown: waits, hang-ups, referrals, or perhaps an unusual opportunity. Getting around town would ordinarily be difficult, except that Rosa has a car. "My car has more rights than me. For fifty dollars my car can live in that garage across the street. In fact, it can even live right here on the curb, but I can't," she says. Sheila, standing aside, has just asked Rosa for a ride to an apartment about a mile away. She and her seven-year-old daughter, who has attended eleven schools already, have just received a Section 8 certificate that qualifies her for housing. "I suppose that I should be happy" she says. "I've waited eight months, but most people tell me I won't be able to find a landlord that will take it. Anyway, I've started a list. It's good for thirty days."

In Detroit, Arch has always been single and a working man for most of his thirty-three adult years. "I don't have no friends. I really haven't in a long time," he says while his eyes scan the remnants of neighborhood tenement buildings that are ninety years old. "I sometimes hear them saying that I've got the v's, y'know, the lines on the back of your neck. It's supposed to mean that you don't have much time," he says, sensing the reality of his typical life expectancy. Arch will return to a "fancy" SRO tonight, a notable exception recently due in part to the government's redefinition of a long-standing medical condition, which now gives him some additional money to be able to afford a "real home" in a cheap hotel. "But that could change, like it did back in '82, when they cut my SSI money. The Feds told me one day that I didn't qualify anymore."

Rosa, Sheila, Arch, and all the others wonder about receiving mail, storing valuables, and preparing for a job interview. They wonder about family that is out of contact, and how to avoid troublemakers or the truly dangerous. Sheila wonders if she and her daughter can go to the bathroom when they need to and "when they can take a long time, and go in private." And they wonder about the remaining time in the rest of the day.

Finally, as the evening approaches, homeless people must find suitable shelter. Frank and John T. will return to the shelter the same as they have for the last month. Tent City residents will remain for several more days until all sides feel that the point is made. Rosa will sleep in her car, a departure from the ordinary, after spending a long day looking for apartments. Sheila and her daughter will impose one more time upon her aunt, who has an extra bedroom. Arch will return to his fancy SRO, but Billy, who has been denied shelter on previous occasions, will not likely seek any ordinary lodging tonight. Since adequate shelter is limited in most cities, finding a place to stay may be a product of chance or time and place. It may also be unacceptable in a variety of ways, ranging from the physical conditions of the dwelling to the nature of the people with whom they must associate.

These composites are derived from the real lives and experiences of homeless people in our society. Although tomorrow the names may change and the stories may vary, it presents to us a disturbing and twisted portrait of an America that, for most of us, is unimaginable. It is no doubt difficult for most of us to imagine being homeless in a society where so much of our lives is somehow connected to home. It may also be difficult to understand exactly what all of these people are talking about. Not only do homeless people lead lives very different from most of the rest of us, but they often speak what may seem to be a different language. Special phrases and terms such as "SRO," "section 8," and even "shelter" are likely to be unfamiliar to us. These scenes also reflect, to a certain extent, the different kinds of people that are homeless today, the different places that they may stay, and some examples of their daily experiences.

Homeless people have difficulty getting through the day in any normal sense of the term. They have problems getting from one place to another because of the lack of an automobile or even, perhaps, a license to drive. Normal buying habits are seriously altered because of the necessity of carrying sufficient cash at all times. Many are without a checking account or a credit card. Registering for a class or a training program is extremely cumbersome or even impossible without an address. And of course finding out if they qualify for a job or a class is harder since they probably do not receive mail in any ordinary way. Even the prospect of applying for a job is made more difficult when these various conditions must be revealed to a potential employer.

If you have had the opportunity to read or hear about the homeless you may be able to add some specific examples to each of the scenes depicted above to create an even more complex picture of a day in the life of a homeless person. Meanwhile, many Americans make judgments, sometimes negative, about these people. Their expressions reveal much of what they are thinking once they see homeless people and many are uncomfortable being nearby. And perhaps we can now begin to sense why many preconceived notions about the homeless obscure the true nature of a complex problem.

Experts, policy-makers, and ordinary people disagree about the causes of homelessness and recommendations for its solution. But there are common elements that have contributed to homelessness that we can describe and study to begin to understand why the problem persists in such a wealthy nation as the United States. To begin to understand the problem, experts have attempted to count homeless people and to assess their characteristics. They have also studied the streets, the shelters, and the many agencies that somehow precariously link the homeless person with society. Who the homeless are and where they live is the topic of Chapter 2, Homelessness: People and Places.

All of the individuals discussed in our examples above share in the culture of the United States, but in some ways different from our experiences. Because of severe material lack, they often have to make choices or alter their expectations in ways that you and I have not been required to do. On the other hand, their ideas about fairness and decency are probably quite similar to other Americans. Because homeless people have acquired a label, a set of expectations have been established for them and a picture of them has been formed in our minds. Our cultural beliefs and values are likely to cause us to ask about their employment and their prospects of getting ahead. We might wonder if their lives would be different if they had worked harder or if they created many of their own problems. We might even hear public officials expressing these same ideas and suggesting that the problem would largely disappear if people would act in a more responsible manner. Because national and local policy decisions are made by people who have learned certain cultural ideas about such things as success and responsibility, it is important for us to examine these ideas. How can our beliefs, attitudes, and values influence the nature of homelessness in our society today? In what ways are policy decisions affected by our prevailing cultural patterns? We will examine some of our most important cultural patterns as they relate to the condition of homelessness in Chapter 3, the

Culture of Homelessness.

Culture becomes "real" only when we interact with other people and define them in relation to us. Ordinarily, this definition is based upon the most important or visible qualities that are noted; it could be tragic if that definition is not a positive or pleasant one. We might assume, for example, that homeless people are inclined to act in certain ways because they are homeless. We might also assume that there is a cause-effect relationship between two elements that we observe together. For example, we might assume that a person who drinks and is homeless is an alcoholic and that his alcoholism is the cause of his homelessness. These kinds of judgements that we make may become common and practiced by those people who develop policies to deal with homelessness. We will examine some of the common ways that the causes of homelessness have been defined and what actions have been taken in past years to attempt to remedy the problem. This will be discussed in Chapter 4, The Causes of Homelessness.

Homelessness enters our lives and places of business in an increasingly frequent manner. People are disturbed about the condition of homelessness and want something done. It is clear that efforts that have been made in the past have not been sufficient to correct the problem. It is also quite clear that the problem is becoming more and more a major object of national attention. In recent years, significant advocacy efforts such as protests and law suits have challenged some traditional methods of dealing with the problem. And contemporary in-depth studies of homelessness and many related issues have led to a clearer understanding of the problem and the necessary policy changes that must be made. What should be our social policies toward homelessness, and what are the prospects or recommendations for the future? This will be the topic of Chapter 5, Homelessness: Policies and Prospects.

You will also notice numerous special discussions and charts that will focus on certain aspects of homelessness and exemplify the themes of each chapter.

Chapter Two
Homelessness: People and Places

The ten homeless people who were profiled in the previous chapter represent a wide variety of social catagories. They include families, minorities, working people, and children. Five of them were sheltered for a night in more or less conventional ways. Frank and John T. stayed in two of the thousands of beds available in shelters in U.S. cities today. Arch stayed in his SRO, a term used to describe a "single room occupancy" in a cheap hotel. Shelia and her daughter stayed with a relative for "one more night". Four others-Rosa, Lionel, Veralina, and her son-slept in socially unacceptable, though temporarily tolerable places such as a car or a tent. Billy, who slept under a freeway overpass, was unsheltered.

Who are the homeless and where are they found? Although there are many different conditions of homelessness, the central issues of today's homelessness problem concerns the total number of people involved and how these people are different from homeless people of the past. In recent years, homelessness has ranked among our most serious urban problems. Some observers have claimed that it represents the most significant national crisis since the Great

Depression. And compared to other countries, no other modern industrial nation suffers from such a widespread malady.

Homelessness in the distant past. Has homelessness always been a problem? In one sense, yes. But because of historical changes in what is considered an obligation of society, today's homelessness is particularly significant.

Historically, societies have been characterized by extreme inequalities in the distribution of wealth, prestige, and power. Prior to industrialization, agriculture was the main product of a society, and wealth accompanied land ownership. Typically, a very small percent of the population would own most of the land. In contrast, the living conditions of peasants were austere, and it is doubtful that they were as well off as hunters and gatherers had been thousands of years earlier. Household furnishings were extremely simple and basic. A few stools, a table, and a chest might be all; beds were rare and people usually slept on the floor.

Migration to cities from rural areas marked a significant change in a person's social network. For individuals, the family represented economic opportunity and support, but many were not able to maintain a farm. Quite often the impoverished would take to the road for good, drifting about with the floating population of homeless people which included several million people in Europe by the 1780s. Life for these people was, as the English political philosopher Thomas Hobbes put it, "nasty, brutish and short." Working conditions for unskilled laborers were dangerous and injuries were common. A worker might be able to work only a few years, after which he could survive only by begging or by becoming a criminal. Estimates of the number of beggars ranged from one-tenth to one-third of the urban population. For these people, shelter became increasingly difficult to obtain. Homelessness, then, was often a fine line that divided primitive shelter from none at all.

Immigration to the United States, which began in the early 1600s, often included many people who were from the poorest segments of society. It was probably from this group that the first homeless Americans appeared. English Poor Laws of the time required local communities to support needy and dependent persons. However, many communities made it difficult for nonworking newcomers to settle. Many were warned out or told to move beyond the town's borders. Nonmembers of towns could apply for either membership or permission to become a public charge but they were not likely to be granted stays unless there was a probability that they would become self-supporting. Punishments for those who tried to stay could be harsh. Thus, a colonial group of wandering poor was created, moving from town to town seeking some kind of permanent settlement.

Although many homeless likely found shelter with relatives, others would board temporarily with families who might receive a small payment from the community. Gradually institutions, soup kitchens, and even some temporary public shelters were built beginning in the 18th century, but it was debated whether improving conditions would destroy homeless people's initiative to work by providing them with cheap housing. Nevertheless, by 1850, the state of New York had almshouses, which sheltered some ten thousand people, or the equivalent of more than seventy thousand today. Approximately one-fourth were children and many suffered from various disabilities. Crowded and unsanitary conditions were common (Caton, p.6).

Terms of help were normally highly dependent upon length of settlement for most poor people, a stipulation that persisted, at least partially, until the 1960s. The Civil War created conditions unlike those of previous times that led to a considerable increase in the number of homeless and the first recognition of a national problem. Many veterans joined immigrants and sought jobs as railroad workers or obtained other mobile, seasonal occupations often connected to the growth of the Industrial Revolution. Mostly these workers were young and unattached, but they were often literate and had job skills. It was during this time that the term "hobo" probably originated in response to where one was headed. The answer was "*ho*meward *bo*und." Hoboes, or migratory workers, normally distinguished themselves from "tramps," or migratory nonworkers who were generally considered to be "barbarians openly at war with society" (Hopper, p.161). To others, *tramp* is a generic term that refers to transients who share a common culture based upon particular survival needs. As America's population and diversity grew, the traditional image of the homeless person as a moral failure, an idle vagrant, and a threat to honest labor became increasingly dissociated from the facts.

The next expansion of the homeless population was a product of the Great Immigration and the subsequent growth of urban areas. Between 1870 and 1924 some twenty-three million persons immigrated to America seeking a job and a place to settle. The population of New York City, which passed one million in 1875, quickly grew to three and a half million by 1900. These new immigrants were crowded into forty-three thousand dark, stuffy, and dirty tenement houses (Novotny, p. 136); estimates of the number of families that would experience homelessness were one in five (Hoch, p.20). The prevailing lack of sympathy for the homeless and the absence of any public assistance meant that every poor family, and some middle class families too, found themselves one personal or economic crisis away from destitution. But instead of strengthening the safety net, public fear of a potential tramp problem led to the passage of various state Tramp Laws that were intended to replace shelters with imprisonment. However, the criminalization of the tramp population did not diminish their numbers, particularly during the frequent economic recessions. By the end of the century, tramps ordinarily had two options for shelter: privately operated *rescue missions*, which required attendance at religious services and sometimes a small donation, and municipal *lodging houses*, or squalid residential warehouses that offered a bunk with little privacy in exchange for manual labor. As the traditional family became less common as a result of industrialization and increased mobility, family responsibility for destitution became increasingly more difficult to maintain. The changing nature of social life required a redefinition of the idea of helping the homeless. In an industrial society where large numbers of people are separated from their families, the only institution capable of maintaining consistant care must be the government. But neither federal or local governments responded sufficiently to meet the increased needs.

The development of skid row. On a corner along Yesler Street in Seattle, Washington, a bronze plaque notes the origin of the original "skid row." According to local historians, Skid Road was aptly named for the street where logs were skidded down to Henry Yesler's sawmill and where poor people lived among the brothels and saloons. Similar skid rows were becoming a common sight in large cities during the latter part of the 19th century as a large body of transient workers became victims of frequently-recurring economic recessions. For example, following the Panic of 1873, unemployment rates escalated to thirty or forty percent. During the Panic of 1893 unemployment was estimated as between nine hundred thousand and three million, or about one out of every seven or eight men (Caton, p.8).

Gradually, the homeless problem became the target of serious study. Surveys and in-depth interviews of hundreds of homeless persons by researchers such as McCook in 1893, Solenberger in 1911, and Anderson in 1923 began to reveal many details previously unrecognized. Homelessness was found to be primarily a consequence of unemployment and not of immoral living, and many homeless people were found to be relatively young and literate and had job skills. Among the most important findings were details related to health. It was discovered that many suffered from major health problems such as blindness, deafness, or other physical disabilities. About one in ten had tuberculosis and another eleven percent had serious mental disorders. Anderson, a former transient worker who became a sociologist, concluded that seasonal or mobile workers would end up jobless and homeless because they were no longer "industrially adequate" due to physical, mental, and family problems (Caton, p.9).

Homelessness during the Great Depression. When the Great Depression of the 1930s began, the number of homeless, which had remained relatively constant in previous decades, grew significantly. Cities experienced massive unemployment: fifty percent of Cleveland's working people were unemployed; sixty percent in Akron and eighty percent in Toledo (Spates, p.126). The Federal Transient Bureau in 1933 estimated the number of transient and homeless persons to be approximately 1 to 1.5 million; other estimates ranged from 2 to 5 million out of a U.S. population of some 123 million, equivalent to considerably more than twice the number of homeless today. Many drifted to the skid rows of larger cities where they found it increasingly difficult to find affordable housing. Flophouses, ordinarily the cheapest option, usually charged twenty-five cents a night, but even that was more than many unemployed people could afford at a time when the minimum wage was only thirty-five cents per hour. It was during this time that the Federal Emergency Relief Administration (FERA) was established and set up camps for transient workers. Many homeless people worked on public works projects such as repairing roads or clearing forests during the two-year existence of this agency. Researchers also began to record the emergence of a new homeless group consisting of families like the Joads in John Steinbeck's *The Grapes of Wrath*. These victims of circumstance generated some public sympathy greater than that afforded the typical skid row residents, but not much. For example, the state of California actually barricaded its border entrances with Highway Patrol officers and National Guardsmen and refused to allow people without visible means of support admission to the Golden State. This illegal action, which lasted only a matter of days, nevertheless indicated the lack of official sympathy for the homeless.

In larger cities, typical homeless shelters were often formerly vacant buildings converted by public relief agencies into dormitories. Residents slept in cots and had access to toilet and bathing facilities. Recreation rooms were sometimes provided and two meals were generally served. Families often set up temporary "squatter settlements" on the periphery of cities sometimes called "Hoovervilles" in mock recognition of the President of the United States. In smaller towns and in rural areas, little is known of how homeless people fared, although local homeless were more likely to receive assistance than transients. Eventually World War II greatly reduced the number of homeless through military service and war industry opportunities.

Profile:
Hood River Blackie, Hobo Historian

Ralph Gooding became a hobo in 1940 at the age of fourteen when he left home after his father threw a pitchfork at him. He picked up his nickname from a town in Oregon where he picked apples and spent his next thirty-three years on the road. "It seems like just last summer that I jungled up behind the old icehouse at Wenatchee with Chicken Red, Joe Brophy, and Tex Medders".

But Blackie was more than just another wandering hobo, for he began, when he was young, to chronicle his life and the lives of Bughouse McCann, Lying Roy Livingston, Old Watermelon Red, Scissors Sam and hundreds of other old-time hoboes. Blackie has given Columbia University's History Department diaries, notes, and fourteen hours of tape recordings on some 611 hoboes that he came in contact with while riding the rails. He wrote a book, *The Passing of the Hobo*, and for a while worked as a historian for the

California Parks and Recreation Department, developing the hobo history section at the State Railroad Museum in Sacramento.

"The old-time hobo wore his home on his back and had no intentions of settling down, except perhaps at the Salvation Army kitchen for a little soup and religion - usually in that order of preference. They would hang together as tight as any fraternal lodge and would share everything down to their last slice of bologna."

When he entered his fifties, he finally quit the tracks because "the new breed didn't absorb the culture." Despite having only an eighth-grade education, he settled into his new life writing about unknown Americans and appearing on TV documentaries. But he still preferred the jungle and "some fresh-cooked Mulligan stew." Blackie, along with Feather River John and Steam Train Maury, also wanted to establish a low budget "retirement camp" for elderly hoboes. "Once you've lived a life on the rails, 'lights off at ten o'clock' is tough to take."

Hood River Blackie died in 1983

(Sacramento Bee, Feb. 6, 1983)

After the war, the growth of the economy and general prosperity resulted in some observers actually predicting the end of homelessness and poverty as serious problems. According to these optimists, as the economic boom continued and new social services were provided, the old skid rows would naturally decline. In 1950, it was estimated that there were only 150,000 homeless in all the nation's largest cities (Ropers, p.92). It was during this time that researchers focused their attention on the conditions of the city areas where the homeless lived and speculated about the effects of urban renewal programs on deteriorating city environments.

During the 1950s, homelessness was usually defined as living apart from a family. But typically, some kind of shelter, though meager, was available. One researcher described Chicago's flophouses as having windowless rooms about five by seven feet, each with a single light bulb, walls that did not quite reach to the ceiling, and renting for fifty to ninety cents per night (Rossi, p.30). Rescue missions provided additional space and only a few were living outdoors. One sociologist who studied Chicago in 1958 counted only 110 men living in the streets. Another sociologist, studying Philadelphia's skid row in 1960, counted only sixty-four persons living in the streets, although it is unclear if these figures represented an accurate count of the total homeless population. Part of the reason for the small numbers can be explained by increased police arrests for public drunkenness and other similar crimes, which, in larger cities, accounted for some twenty-five percent of all arrests (Rossi, p.31). Typical homeless residents during the 1950s were older men, often averaging fifty years of age and often suffering from one or more impediments such as alcoholism, mental illness, or a physical disability. Social isolation was usually mentioned as characteristic of these homeless persons - virtually none were married and most had no one they considered a good friend.

Urban renewal programs during the 1950s were designed to allow cities to battle urban decline. A local government could define a neighborhood or region as blighted, force owners to sell and, in turn, resell the property to private developers for profitable redevelopment. Typically, poor neighborhoods were targeted for urban renewal projects and although many public-use projects were built, the housing that was reconstructed was often not affordable to the former residents of the area. This pattern was repeated frequently in the 1960s and critics labeled the process as an effort to remove poor people and minorities from neighborhoods with economic potential for the middle class. Considering the declining number of persons defined as homeless, their typical older age profile, the increasing vacancy rates among cheap hotels, and the increased mechanization of low-skill jobs, it is not surprising that many researchers and politicians advocated a desire to clean up the slums of the cities.

Homelessness today. Beginning in the 1970s homeless activists and shelter providers began to note an increase in the homeless population although the profile was confusing at first. Because of the decriminalization of public drunkenness and a decrease in arrests for other related violations such as vagrancy, more homeless people who were formerly in jails began to regularly appear on the street. The increase of recently released patients from state mental institutions left many former inmates on their own still suffering from mental illness. In addition, there was a significant increase in the number of women who, in years past, rarely accounted for more than five percent of the visible homeless population. Finally, homeless families began to appear and a more complicated picture of homelessness began to emerge. One image included people who were "dirty, wore torn or inappropriate clothing, hallucinated or shouted to others, and in general acted in a strange or bizarre way" (Caton, p.12). At the same time, a different image was presented to the public- the image of a family breadwinner who lost his job in a factory and after weeks of searching for jobs not to be found, packed the family and their possessions into an aging car only to arrive in a city with no opportunities or cash. Considering the impact that the post-war economic boom years had on shaping Americans' views of success and upward mobility, it was hard for many to understand such an increase in homelessness in terms other than personal failure. Even the most sympathetic cases seemed to be an isolated exception to our beliefs about American opportunity. In addition, the political themes of the 1980s suggested that there were not very many homeless, and most were probably to blame for their condition.

A profile of the homeless. Due to the dramatic increase in homelessness in the 1970s and 1980s, research and public attention was increasingly drawn to what was being called a national crisis.

Today, there has emerged a profile of homelessness that is more accurate and precise than at any other time in history. Yet, there are enormous difficulties in estimating the number of homeless and their characteristics. Since homeless people cannot be counted in the same way that housed people can, estimates and samples must be relied upon. Even shelters cannot offer an accurate yearly estimate since their population changes daily. Also, many homeless people on the streets are not distinguishable from other people and still others will attempt to avoid being counted. Even government efforts to estimate the total number of homeless may be flawed. According to sociologist Richard Appelbaum in his testimony to a congressional subcommittee attempting to understand the government's own efforts to count the homeless in 1984, "the report suffers from methodological deficiencies which cast serious doubt on the validity of its conclusions" (Appelbaum, p.156). The government study neglected to discuss possible methodological difficulties and initially did not provide access to its data to allow other researchers to attempt to validate the results. Even the Census Bureau was unable to accurately estimate the total number of homeless in the 1990 Census. Bureau of Census officials, working in teams and using flashlights to illuminate their questionnaires, attempted to count every homeless person that they could find during the night of March 20 and 21. Their estimate of 228,621 is considered quite low by experts. In contrast, a 1988 study by the National

Alliance to End Homelessness estimated some 735,000 homeless on a given night in the U.S. And homeless advocate Mitch Snyder repeatedly claimed that there were three million homeless. These estimates, and others, suggest that such a wide disparity in numbers is the result of the special difficulties associated with the counting of homeless people and possibly the differing intent of the counters.

Respected estimates of the total number of homeless in America suggest that there are somewhere between about 650,000 and one million persons on any given night. Recent studies and estimates, including ones by the Urban Institute, the U.S. Conference of Mayors, the U.S. Department of Education, and various sociologists and practitioners, all produce different numbers and groupings, often depending upon the researchers' intent or the self-imposed parameters of their research. Other estimates by those who are more likely to be biased place the numbers considerably higher or lower. Potentially, the total number could be much higher than the 650,000 to one million estimate; researchers believe that the number of homeless in a year may be two or possibly even three times greater than the number on any given night. In addition, the total could become much higher if unpredictable or sudden difficulties forced many of the people at high risk of becoming homeless out of their dwellings. If the ratio of one night's count to annual estimates of homelessness is accurate, and if those vulnerable to homelessness were forced from their housing, then it is possible that homelessness could easily include millions of people in a given year. Therefore, selecting a set of numbers and dividing the estimates into catagories to produce a profile of the homeless is always a best guess effort. What does such a profile look like?

Homeless *families* account for about twenty to thirty-five percent of all homeless people. Part of the reason for the wide range of the estimate is due to differing definitions of what constitutes a family. About twenty to twenty-five percent of all homeless are *children*. Many of these families are headed by *single mothers* although about one-fourth of them are not likely to actually have their children living with them. These younger women are likely to be potentially employable if day care were available. Approximately one-half receive welfare. Since the children are distributed among a variety of caretakers, most homeless children live in broken families. According to researchers, these children will suffer from a variety of physical disorders at a rate two to ten times greater than children in the general population. The number of two-parent homeless families is unclear, with an estimated range of about one percent to over twenty-three percent. Again, differences in defining this group result in different estimates. This catagory is often portrayed in the media as the new homeless.

Single persons make up the remaining four-fifths of the homeless population. About eight to thirteen percent of this group are women and about five percent are children, typically older "throwaways" living alone on the streets. There are similar numbers of male and female minors and the rate of pregnancy is probably one in four.

About fifty to seventy percent of the homeless population are *single adult males* that have no clear family ties. Relatively few are older, perhaps three percent, which is considerably smaller than the same age group in the general population. It is likely that a high mortality rate accounts, in part, for the small size of the older group. It is also possible that some older people's social security payments may provide just enough to avoid homelessness. The striking characteristic of the adult males, in contrast to typical tramp populations of years ago, is their relatively young typical age of thirty-five. Part of the explanation may be the result of the large baby boom generation that was born during the 1946-1964 period. Single homeless males are likely to have been homeless and jobless longer than any other homeless subgroup. Although one half have completed high school, most have been institutionalized for either criminal offenses, mental illness, or chemical dependency treatment. About twenty percent of single males have never had any of these experiences. Minorities represent a larger proportion of this group, and other homeless groups as well, as compared to the general population. Many of these single adult men are without relatives and often lived alone before becoming homeless. A sizable number, about twenty-five to thirty percent, of the single males are *veterans*, which is similar to the total percent of veterans in the general population. However, Vietnam veterans are overrepresented. About one in five Vietnam veterans have serious service-related disabilities, which would make them more vulnerable to unemployment and other difficulties.

Approximately twelve to thirty percent of the total homeless population are seriously mentally ill; perhaps as many as forty percent are considered to be substance abusers. In fact, generally poor health is reported by homeless people at a rate some three times higher than that of the general population. It is important to realize that poor health can be either a condition that led to homelessness or one that resulted from it.

It is possible that a small number of able-bodied males with no serious impairments can be found among the homeless population, but the proportion would probably be small, perhaps five percent. This is the group that critics often publicly denounce as inappropriate recipients of misguided government giveaway programs. However, about twenty percent of all homeless males are working full or part time, or are actively seeking work.

Researchers have often developed distinctions among different kinds of poor people so as to better understand the nature of homelessness. *Poverty*, as defined by the federal government, afflicts those persons falling below certain income levels, such as about $14,000 annually for a family

PERSONS BELOW POVERTY LEVEL

YEAR	PERCENT BELOW	MILLIONS OF POOR	INCOME STANDARD*
1960	22.0	39.9	$3022
1965	17.0	33.2	$3223
1970	13.0	25.4	$3968
1975	12.0	25.9	$5500
1980	13.0	29.3	$8414
1985	14.0	33.1	$10,989
1990	13.5	33.6	$13,359
1991	14.2	35.7	$13,924

*Income Standard based upon a family of four

Source: U.S. Bureau of the Census, Current Population Reports

of four in 1993. Accordingly, there are approximately thirty-five million poor people, or about one in seven of the population of the United States who would be considered poor by this definition. *Homelessness,* or the lack of permanent shelter, is generally found among the poorest poor people where life is extremely precarious. There is, in addition, another group of poor people who are sometimes labelled *marginally homeless,* or who are in great risk of becoming homeless. If we compare these groups with one another there may be one homeless person for every thirty-five to fifty poor people today. It would be very hard to estimate what percent of the poverty population is at very great risk of becoming homeless but it may be at least fifteen percent. On the other hand, if housing costs alone were an indication of great risk, about eighty percent of all poor people pay more rent than they should according to the federal government's affordable housing standards.

Where do all of these people stay? Years ago, tramps would often compile mental lists of places to flop in each city that they would visit. For example, Spradley discovered hundreds of categories of flops, including "empty building, weed patch, railroad flop, mission flop, car flop, window well, all-night laundromat, furnace room, bus depot, stairwell, park bench, loading dock" and many others (Spradley, p.111). But today, many of these flops would not be considered acceptable, appropriate, or safe to many of the homeless who now include families, women, and children.

Today, the housing possibilities for homeless people are quite varied, and sometimes the result of innovative action by both the homeless and their providers. The following categories will give us examples of the different kinds of places.

Shelters consist of a wide variety of temporary living facilities including large buildings, such as armories or warehouses, that have been converted to dorm-style living facilities for dozens or even hundreds or more people. It may also refer to a network of smaller, specialized residences scattered throughout a city. Sometimes, in large cities, comprehensive services are provided, including job referrals, benefits counseling, and health services. Funding is usually provided by non-profit corporations or private groups. Generally they have a mixed reputation among clients. Shelters may also refer to *rescue missions*, which are usually affiliated with a church or religious organization. Examples of shelters would include the Bowery Mission in New York City (which advertises itself as "an open door since 1879"), the Salvation Army, and the St. Vincent De Paul/Joan Kroc Center in San Diego, which serves more than a thousand people a day.

Profile:
An Exemplary Homeless Shelter

The brand new, $11.6 million St. Vincent De Paul- Joan

Kroc Center in San Diego opened its doors to the homeless in August, 1987. It houses 350 people, serves 1,350 meals daily, has a full medical clinic, and a large staff of professionals and volunteers. The three-story building has top-of-the-line furnishings, a children's day care center, a permanent elementary school, and a 15,000 square foot courtyard with benches, landscaping, pillars, and a fountain.

The facility was designed as a transitional center for homeless people who are in the process of stabilizing their lives as they attempt to move to a permanent life off the streets. Electronic credit card key locks secure residents' rooms, cameras survey public areas, and security guards patrol around the clock. New residents are ordinarily referred by other social agencies, appointments are made, and intake interviews develop a detailed plan to get the homeless person a home and a job. The counselor assigned to each case helps develop reasonable goals with the new client that will lead to "graduation," typically in six months. It is the policy of the center to direct the full force of its resources toward those who will most likely succeed.

Many short term services are also provided, including a Day Center that provides basic personal and appearance needs, meals, and referrals. The center provides office space for a county welfare worker, a consumer credit counselor, and other representatives of social service agencies. A Resource Center contains phones, typewriters, a copy machine, an answering machine for employment and housing callbacks, and ongoing seminars in job coaching.

Funding comes from a variety of individual donors and special events as well as Federal and local sources. New programs or plans include a comprehensive food network, a farm facility, and additional buildings for more shelter.

(Coates, pp.114-123)

Transitional housing is intended to help people with special needs. This often includes abused women with children, substance abusers or people with other special problems. The intent is to provide the groundwork for an eventual transition to normal housing arrangements. Facilities may be made available for several weeks to a year or more. Sometimes job training programs are conducted and residents may work in exchange for the benefits. An example of transitional housing can be found at the St. Anthony's Foundation Farm in Northern California

---

Profile:
St. Anthony's Farm

Transitional housing is an important step in stabilizing the lives of homeless people. St. Anthony's Foundation of San Francisco has, for the last 30 years, managed a farm program to help homeless men "find a temporary haven from society" in order to gain a new perspective on their lives. According to Vic Allcorn, who oversees the 350-acre farm some 50 miles north of the city, the foundation's primary goals are to help the 40 residents reestablish basic living standards and identify their feelings about themselves and their coworkers. In addition, the staff of 13 helps to administer an ongoing program directed toward resolving substance abuse problems. An ethnically diverse population, averaging about 30 years of age, works in a variety of jobs including caring for the 4,000 hogs and the 350 dairy cattle that produce 1,000 gallons of milk per day. A long-term goal is to return the acreage to food production so as to meet the needs of San Francisco's St. Anthony's Dining Hall, which serves more than 1,000 urban homeless daily. Residents, most of whom have had a long history of homelessness and related problems, typically stay four months at the farm and then move to a foundation-operated urban residence hall. There, they will slowly attempt to establish "a clean and sober network" outside of St. Anthony's.

St. Anthony's Dining Hall

SROs are an acronym for single room occupancy units typically found in older downtown hotels. In the past, they were often referred to as flophouses or flea bags. Rooms are usually small, may have no windows, and residents usually share bathroom facilities. Sometimes residents may simply rent a bed in a room shared with many others. Normally privately operated for profit, they have diminished in number in recent years due to urban renewal and other economic and political reasons.

A variety of other residential units in the open market are often sought by homeless people, including privately-owned low-income apartments or houses, garages, or other residential dwellings that may have been converted legally or otherwise; transitional buildings that are in the process of being condemned or abandoned; and special housing units that are a part of a service including abused women's shelters, substance abuse units, and church-owned residences. Less desirable places could include parks, vacant lots, freeway overpass areas, excavated sites in building projects, cars (sometimes for rent), abandoned vehicles, and numerous other places often known only by the desperate.

In addition to shelter for the night, many other aspects of housing are needed by homeless people during the day. Perhaps the most worrisome need that arises is the search for a convenient restroom. The needs for the use of a toilet and for necessary cleaning and general appearance preparations are critical yet difficult to find. For ten years, the city of San Diego debated the necessity of providing *one* additional public restroom in the downtown area that would join the city's single other public restroom. Now, the city proclaims that an average of 344 "event-free" uses occur daily in this one newly constructed restroom, not including washing (Coates, p 208). Recently, New York and other cities have begun to provide street kiosk-style automatic toilets similar to those that have been common in the streets of Paris for years. Additional needs of homeless people include affordable meals in sheltered locations, mail delivery, and safe and inexpensive storage facilities.

There is no doubt that there is a severe lack of acceptable and appropriate housing for homeless people. The shortage of various living arrangements is compounded by the lack of public facilities and the often overextended private charities. Why this condition has persisted as a serious problem since the mid-1970s is a product of our nation's social and cultural ideas, and their subsequent translation into policies shaped by various communities and governments over the years. In the next chapters, we will examine these social and cultural patterns.

Chapter Three
The Culture of Homelessness

All the homeless people that we discussed in the beginning chapter share an understanding of what it means to be without a home. When Rosa states that her car has more rights than she does, it reveals an understanding of the unique legal status that many homeless people must confront. When Sheila mentions that she has just received a Section 8 certificate, it means that she has qualified for a type of rent supplement that requires an understanding of some complex bureaucratic procedures. And when Arch comments about the unpredictability of SSI, he demonstrates an understanding of a particular type of Social Security payment that is subject, over the years, to political redefinition. Although ordinary people may not readily understand these conversations, homeless people understand each other because they share a "culture of homelessness." But the culture of homelessness touches our lives, too. Each of us have ideas about homelessness and its causes and solutions. How did we develop these ideas and what are their origins?

Houses and Homes. Being homeless is an extremely difficult condition for us to imagine in a country where most of our daily lives are somehow connected to home. Our home is often the center of our personal lives, the place where we interact with others, and an important extension of our cultural selves. Home is, of course, where the heart is, where we nest while watching home videos or home shopping and where children go for home schooling. We spend time in Home Depot, travel back along the home stretch, raise homeboys and worry about being a homebody. This picture is a product of our cultural image of home, home ownership, and all that is implied with permanent residency.

Notice that we are not discussing "the houseless." In fact, most of us will make a distinction between house and home that is more than a semantic difference. In our culture, the idea of one's home suggests more than just a building:

> A *home* offers a sense of security, of permanence, of one's own space. In fact, where we live, where we are from, is often the quintessential source of our self-identity. Perhaps the defining characteristic of homelessness, which often is ignored, is the homeless person's total lack of support - physical, financial, emotional, spiritual (King, p.8).

This distinction between house and home is a critical one, for it requires us to look beyond simple shelter arrangements and to consider the broader implications of what it means to live in an orderly way in society today. What are some of the critical distinctions between home and mere shelter?

Imagine for a moment the front door ritual. A knock and a "come in" defines the idea of *control and accessibility*. We are exercising a fundamental right to grant permission to others to enter a predefined territory. The territory may be a house, a room, or even an area. Those of you who have shared a room with a brother or sister while growing up may recall various incidents where territory was violated or when lines of chalk or tape were fixed to the floor or wall to precisely define, forever, each person's own personal space. When we control access, we define who we wish to associate with and who we wish to exclude. Control and accessibility allow us the relative freedom of culturally defining a place as home.

Controlling access also implies the existence of *privacy*, which along with comfort, may be the two most desired home requirements today. Whether privacy implies sleeping, eating, bathing, or simply, privacy for thought, the net effect is the ability to withdraw at will from the common life of one's surroundings.

Control and privacy are ultimately a product of official recognition. We have a right to be there, or, in other words, we believe in *secure tenure*. Secure tenure may be granted specifically by a law, or by someone in authority, or even by custom if a collective sense of right of occupancy exists. Secure tenure protects us from those who would arbitrarily or through the use of power require us to leave. We have the means to defend our right to be there. Secure tenure does not, however, imply permanence. If you were to ask your neighbors the simple question, "Do you plan to leave or do you plan to stay?", they would likely have little trouble answering. People usually enter a neighborhood with expectations about the future of their residence. But even those neighbors who indicate that their stay will be temporary will have strong feelings about secure tenure. They believe they have a right to be there.

Control, privacy, and secure tenure are possible only when one defines a place, but just any building would not qualify. An important distinction between an ordinary building and a home is convenient access to a *communication network,* and the presence of *sufficient space and security*. Most of us require the tools and connections that tie us to the rest of society. We would find it difficult, unlike Henry David Thoreau at Walden Pond, to do without a convenient postal service. Few people would consider a private telephone or safe storage spaces as luxuries. People expect to be able to install locks or other security devices to protect themselves. Many would argue that self protection is among the most fundamental rights that we possess. Other home features, like private bathrooms and kitchens, we normally take for granted. Many of us consider our ability to personalize our homes an important right of occupancy. And, over time, we may become quite attached to the familiarity of the routes, corners, obstacles, and clutter that characterize the uniqueness of our homes.

Now consider how a homeless person must adjust to the absence of these home qualities. The front door ritual now belongs to the shelter provider. Typically, shelters will determine the acceptability of a potential resident, and thus, will control access. In addition, a shelter resident will have virtually no territorial control except for perhaps a small area surrounding a bed. Clearly, homeless people have no control over those with whom they must associate; they cannot exclude other residents. Privacy is almost never possible. Normally, the only time that homeless people may withdraw from their surroundings is by moving to another public area that has fewer people. Although secure tenure may be technically granted to shelter residents, it could be severely limited by a variety of circumstances and it is never granted permanently. Secure tenure does not necessarily bestow acceptability of a shelter, or suggest quality or even minimum standards. Even though housing codes define minimal shelter standards in all cities, they may not be enforced or they may be difficult to apply to specific circumstances. Although a shelter would imply a building of some kind with sanitary facilities, many important components are not necessarily available. For example, many shelters have minimal access to private telephones, adequate storage facilities, private bathrooms, or kitchen facilities. The public nature of these components requires special adjustments by users. And finally, many shelter residents do not feel safe and have limited ability to control safety conditions

It must seem obvious that there is a cultural dichotomy between our common ideals and reverence of "home" and the reality of a million people without one. Is this a recent condition? Are housing needs different today? How have our cultural beliefs and values contributed to our tolerance of these conditions?

Profile: *Shelters in Chicago*

What is an emergency shelter like? Sociologist Peter Rossi studied Chicago's homeless shelters in preparation for his book, *Down and Out in America.* Rossi found that city shelters are typically run by religious private-sector groups with substantial financial subsidies from the city and the state.   Some of the largest and oldest are missions with strong religious themes, while others are more secularized and charitable. All shelter buildings vary in accommodations; only a few were specifically designed and built to be shelters. For example, a major mission shelter used to be a factory and smaller shelters have been built by modifying apartments or small stores. The largest have several hundred beds normally in dormitory arrangements, although small apartments or private rooms are sometimes available. A typical bedroom in a shelter would probably be shared by fifty people. More than 2,000 beds are provided throughout the city.

Residents of all ethnic groups are commonly seen in shelters and usually no one group is likely to numerically dominate a shelter at a given time. But all shelters have standards or restrictions for admission, the most common being gender.

Half of all shelters will accept only men or only women and the rest commonly limit numbers of each according to gender accommodations. There are some specialized juvenile shelters.

Shelters have regular admitting hours but few restrict the length of stay. Residents can and often do return night after night and more than half of the shelters allow stays beyond one year. The fair market rent for a typical one-bedroom apartment in metropolitan Chicago is $543. For people who earn less than about $80 a week, according to Rossi, the only affordable housing is in emergency shelters. Many will require residents to leave at certain times of the day for housekeeping purposes and some request that residents contribute their labor.

Many shelters have rules that bar those that are intoxicated or those acting in potentially unsettling ways. While in the shelter, residents are often requested not to drink, use drugs, smoke, or act in a disruptive manner. Some shelters will bar persons with chronic mental illness. Rossi says that the ideal client should be sober, well mannered, not mentally ill, and clean and neat. Not all fit this ideal, but if they come close, they will likely be admitted.

When asked their opinions of shelters, most residents spoke favorably and gave positive assessments. The major complaint, shared by about half of the residents, concerned the lack of physical safety and the presence of theft. Although far from luxurious, Chicago's shelters are certainly better than the streets.

Housing in the past. Contrary to many contemporary images, home ownership as we

know it today is a fairly recent phenomenon.
People in previous generations lived in simpler
houses in different arrangements, and often did
not own them. Unlike modern suburbia, the
detached house did not normally exist in early
towns, except for the wealthy.

The houses of our ancestors were normally quite
simple and often built by the inhabitants. A house
would likely have a workplace on the ground floor
with a simple kitchen in the rear. Adjacent to the
shop were living quarters, and sometimes, a
dormitory for hired workers. Since the house
often served as a workplace in addition to a
dwelling, the competition for space between
domestic and work needs was considerable.
Sheds, storage bins, garbage, and even small
industry spilled into gardens, walkways, and other
private areas forming an "intimate connection of
industrial and domestic life" that is "the exact
antithesis of the segregated, legally-sterilized
residential quarter of today" (Mumford, p.284).

As industrialization spread throughout Europe
and the United States in the nineteenth and early
twentieth centuries, increased urbanization led to
a great demand for housing. Many cities built
tenement houses, which were apartment buildings,
five to six stories tall, sharing common sidewalls.
These were rapidly constructed and often did not
have even the most basic amenities such as indoor
plumbing. New immigrants must have looked
with horror at the dark, airless rooms where they
would now live.

Here everything seemed dirtier - ashes from the coal-burning stove settled on every surface, and the smoke from the cheap kerosene in the oil lamp blackened the ceiling. Old wallpaper peeled off in patches. In many buildings a communal faucet or pump on the landing was the only source of running water, which had to be heated on the stove (Novotny, p.145).

With high rents and limited resources, the new immigrants crowded together in these inner city tenements. Sometimes several families containing a dozen or more individuals shared a single flat. Social critics began to write extensively about slums in cities in Europe and the United States and questioned why such conditions should persist. The social changes that resulted from the Industrial Revolution meant that many urban families could no longer afford to house themselves in the same basic and simple ways that their agricultural ancestors could. In fact, some critics concluded that the poor would never be able to afford the cost of standard housing. The increased cost of land, building requirements and codes, and a mobile population meant that fewer poor people could afford to either build or own a home. Soon, the cultural ideas defining the source of responsibility for housing assistance began to slowly shift from family to society.

Modern housing. Most U.S. cities experienced declining housing inventories during the Great Depression and World War II. At the same time internal migration saw some cities facing critical housing shortages. In Washington, D.C., the search for bed and board became an obsession for young men and women drawn to the city as war-related jobs multiplied.

> A woman near 35th and O Streets in Georgetown advertised a basement apartment for seventy-five dollars. Applicants came by the dozens. She interviewed each one in embarrassing detail, inquiring about personal habits of every description - sexual, religious, social, dietary, working, sleeping. But since housing, any housing, was entirely a sellers's market, applicants could refuse to answer her questions only at the risk of having to deal with another landlord even worse - or they could lie (Brinkley, p.233).

Experiences like this in the nation's capital during the Roosevelt years helped lead the federal government, for the first time, into active participation in housing programs. Acting upon recommendations made by housing reform experts years earlier, construction funds were authorized and financial assistance to troubled homeowners facing bank foreclosures was implemented. In the early years of the depression, some 500,000 families were forced to give up their homes due to inability to pay their mortgage (Spates, p.374). The *Federal Housing Administration* (FHA) began operation in 1934 to guarantee new housing loans, and the *Public Works Administration* (PWA) started, in 1938, to hire the unemployed to build public housing in many cities. Housing began to improve, but according to the 1940 Census, some forty percent of the nation's housing lacked major conveniences such as running water. In addition, large public housing projects began to concentrate poor people into inner city islands. Middle-class people began to oppose new construction in their neighborhoods, a response that is commonly referred to as NIMBY or "not in my backyard." When the Supreme Court ruled that public housing authorities could not increase already existing racial segregation by continuing to build in non-white areas, many cities simply stopped building public housing completely (Abu-Lughod, p.228). Other government projects, such as the development of a planned community in Greenbelt, Maryland, designed for working-class families, were attacked by those who felt that government intervention into a privately dominated housing market was too socialistic.

It was not until the postwar housing boom in the late 1940s that rapid construction of new housing began. Developers, including the sons and grandsons of the tenement builders of the 1900s, began to build tract houses in hundreds of places like Levittown, Pennsylvania. With low-interest loans guaranteed by the federal government and newly constructed freeways to the city, the migration to the suburbs began. Many saw Levitt's $8,990 house, with no down payment and monthly payments of only $59, as an opportunity likely never to be repeated. The building of some

3,840 regional shopping malls in a period of only 15 years helped to solidify the popular image of a home on the range only blocks away from any kind of shopping that you would ever want to do. But others began to notice the less desirable aspects of what was sometimes labeled white flight. Many qualified nonwhite buyers were more than surprised when they first read a popular clause in the articles of incorporation of many of these new suburban developments (not including Levittown):

> No person of Negro, Chinese, Japanese, Hindu, Malayan, or Asiatic descent or any other person not of the white or Caucasian race, shall use or occupy said property or any part thereof, except domestic servants, chauffeurs, and gardeners in the employ of white or Caucasian occupants (Lincoln Village Protective Restrictions, p.9).

If suburbanization had a sting, it would be felt in the gradual deterioration of inner cities, which became increasingly the refuge of the minorities and poor people who were unable to take advantage of one of the greatest housing opportunities in our era. If home is where the heart is, then the new heart of America was going to be found in the suburbs. And if we were to try to find a beginning to the contemporary cultural origins of today's homelessness, it could be found in these new suburban settlement patterns.

Who deserves help? Americans will often make distinctions between people who they consider either deserving or unworthy of help. When asked to explain, they may respond in a way that has little to do with actual need. For example, during the post-World War II housing boom, thousands of needy people were denied housing due to their racial classification. To what extent are our current policies for determining the needs of the homeless affected by popular cultural themes?

The ways that we feel about helping the homelessness are derived from significant American cultural ideas that all of us are likely to be exposed to from an early age. Although we live in a very diverse society and speak many different languages, Americans can define, if asked, a set of common values and beliefs that seem to characterize us and set us apart from people in other nations. Understandably, these ideas must be very general in nature to be shared by most Americans, but the very existence of nationhood suggests that there are certain common traits that will bind people together and shape their ideas about success and failure, worthiness, and need. What are some of these ideas?

Survival of the Fittest. Some Americans see society as a jungle where those who are the fittest will succeed in the battle for survival. This "law of nature," as described more than 100 years ago by Herbert Spencer, is sometimes referred to as Social Darwinism. Spencer, who believed that poverty purified society, wrote

...under the natural order of things society

49

is constantly excreting its unhealthy,
imbecile, slow, vacillating, faithless
members, (while) these unthinking, though
well-meaning, men advocate an interference
which not only stops the purifying process,
but even increases the (imperfections) and
absolutely encourages the multiplication of
the reckless and incompetent by offering
them an unfailing provision (Spencer,
p.353).

Although a literal acceptance of Spencer would
seem to be quite un-American today, some might
be inclined to believe in parts and thus judge
others' worthiness for help. For many, a
qualification might be made for those less fit who
are nevertheless deserving because they acquired
a condition through no fault of their own. Others
who are thought to be reckless and incompetent
will likely have greater difficult gaining public
sympathy. Many people still believe that "life is
tough" and that you need to "make your own way."
These Americans are very unlikely to support any
social welfare programs, including housing
assistance for the homeless.

The Promise of Equal Opportunity.
Americans, with few exceptions, believe that
anyone, regardless of background, can rise from
rags to riches, if one is willing to work hard.
Turn-of-the-century author Horatio Alger told
simple tales of poor young men, who with a bit of
pluck and luck took advantage of a golden
opportunity and worked their way to success.

Many similar tales have characterized the American folk tradition of equal opportunity.

Similarly, Americans tend to believe that individual traits such as motivation, a strong sense of achievement, or even intelligence are largely responsible for success or failure. Circumstances beyond the control of the individual are usually given a secondary role except in the most obvious situations. It is clear that an important set of American core values revolves around individualism and self-motivation. Many years ago, generations of school children were taught how to read and how to improve themselves using *The McGuffey Reader:*

> Once or twice though you should fail,
> Try, Try Again;
> If you would, at last, prevail,
> Try, Try Again;
> If we strive, 'tis no disgrace,
> Though we may not win the race;
> What should you do in that case?
> Try, Try Again.
> (Minnich, p.110)

Not living up to one's responsibility to try again and again would be considered a dereliction of one's duty. A *derelict* was a common label attributed to America's homeless population during the 1950s and remained a popular term until the mid-1980s, suggesting that homelessness was largely a problem of lack of effort.

Egalitarianism. Sociologists have commonly listed freedom and equality as major American cultural beliefs. Individual Americans vary considerably with regard to how they interpret the meaning of these ideas. For example, equal opportunity and equality before the law are commonly expressed as fundamental American ideals although considerable debate and ambivalence occur over actual test cases. Another interpretation of egalitarianism advocates the levelling of all inequalities. Although Americans, in general, are not likely to support this position, legal interpretations have, in recent years, often extended equalities to various groups in an attempt to remedy past injustices. For example, mental patients, who had limited rights in years past, have now been granted numerous protections. Critics have pointed out that these protections have had the effect of preventing treatment of those in need who do not consent. In addition, according to one view, what is considered psychotic behavior

> ...might not be present at all, but only an illusion. In this understanding, "craziness" is a term we use to shut away people who are merely different, independent, or eccentric. They listen to a different drummer (Adelson, p.34).

If psychosis is not real, then unusual behavior should not be treated unless the person affected so wishes. By understanding this argument, we can see how the debate over involuntary treatment of the homeless mentally ill has its roots in the extension of egalitarian principles. It may also have influenced decisions leading to the closing of state mental institutions and the release of former patients during the 1960s.

Freedom is also equated with the individual's range of choices. Americans often define freedom as the right to do anything that you want so long as it doesn't hurt anyone else. Although a naive and self-serving interpretation, its logical extension has been the endorsement of a limited governmental role in the regulation of personal affairs. Americans tend to be suspicious and cautious about the intrusion of government programs, and often believe that the private sector can do a better job. Consequently, homeless advocates must overcome extraordinary cultural resistance when attempting to justify greater government assistance.

Group superiority. Prejudice and discrimination have been common cultural themes in American society since its beginning. In fact, sociologist Robin Williams has listed "racism and group superiority themes" as one of the most dominant and important of American value orientations. Common negative sentiments directed against those who differ racially may help to explain the general overrepresentation of minorities among homeless people. It is not a coincidence that minorities represent a larger proportion of the overall homeless population compared to the general population. In addition, these same cultural stereotypes would suggest that services, help, and programs may also be affected by group superiority themes.

The Work Ethic. Work, according to traditional American beliefs, may be more important as an attitude than as a means to put food on the table. In *The Protestant Ethic and the Spirit of Capitalism,* sociologist Max Weber saw a connection between common religious beliefs and our economic behavior. Weber concluded that a branch of the Protestant religion, Calvinism, supplied a spirit or ethic that encouraged the kind of behavior that capitalism expected. Calvinism featured a doctrine that people's lives are determined by the will of God. This doctrine of predestination emphasized that only some people were chosen for salvation and the rest for damnation; neither could alter their fate. Weber suggested that as people tried to determine their future, they began to sense clues or signs of membership among God's chosen people destined for salvation. Important indicators or signs included one's accumulated wealth, thrift, and wise investment - all significant factors in the development of successful capitalism. Many concluded that those who did not possess these qualities of hard work and dedication were not chosen by God for salvation, and thus not deserving of success. As a motivator, the Protestant Ethic was highly successful, since people wished others to believe in their own supposed ultimate salvation. Consequently, work was glorified and became an important measure of a person's life. People in need were often judged according to their worthiness and were differentiated from those who were lazy and careless (Hess, p.66).

Although secularization has diminished the significance of religion in people's lives today, the essential meaning of the work ethic has remained. People try to make sense of their lives in common ways, such as by self-accusation: "It's nobody's fault but mine that I got stuck where I did." If success, then, is due to one's own efforts, then failure must reflect a personal flaw or something lacking within the individual. If those who fail have brought it upon themselves, then the rest of us should not feel any responsibility for their condition. Although most of us would consider the writings of Herbert Spencer to be terribly strict and mean- spirited, perhaps there are still people who would agree in principle with his recommendations that no help, public or private, should be made available to those in need.

Is success partly a result of saving for a rainy day? An important part of the work ethic is postponement of gratification. Early Protestants stressed simplicity and scorn for unnecessary displays of wealth. Those individuals who practiced immediate gratification were viewed as having little self-control and would likely not become successful. Presumably the lack of self-control could be traced to certain character traits, which when practiced, would not lead to success. These traits would form the basis for the "culture of poverty."

The Culture of Poverty. The concept of a culture
of poverty was introduced by anthropologist Oscar
Lewis, who was convinced that poor people in
different countries that he studied shared a
common set of beliefs, attitudes, and values.
These cultural ideas - a design for living within
the constraints imposed by poverty - are passed on
through generations, and limit the individual's
abilities to escape poverty. Lewis felt that by the
time slum children are six or seven they have
usually absorbed the basic values and attitudes of
their subculture and are not psychologically
geared to take full advantage of opportunities that
may occur in their lifetime (Lewis, p.12).

Can an entire culture of poverty be passed on from
generation to generation? Edward Banfield, in his
book *The Unheavenly City*, presents a compelling
though controversial argument on how this process
works. Banfield believes that the explanation lies
in "a psychological orientation toward the future."
Banfield states that

> ...traits that constitute what is called lower-
> class culture of life style are consequences of
> the extreme present-orientation of that
> class. The lower-class person lives from
> moment to moment, he is either unable or
> unwilling to take account of the future or to
> control his impulses. Improvidence and
> irresponsibility are direct consequences of
> this failure to take the future into account...

(and therefore)... he is likely also to be unskilled, to move frequently from one dead end job to another, to be a poor husband and father (Banfield, p.54).

Banfield suggests that lower-class poverty, then, is caused by "ways of thinking and behaving" that are either a part of the personality or deeply ingrained habits. He says that "poverty of this type tends to be self-perpetuating." But Banfield believes that nowadays, poverty is almost always the result of external circumstances - involuntary unemployment, prolonged illness, the death of a breadwinner, or some other misfortune (Banfield, p.142).

Banfield believes that culture of poverty families constitute only a small proportion of the total number of families (perhaps five percent) and perhaps ten to twenty percent of those families below the poverty line. However, he does not help us define which portion of poor people these culture of poverty families are.

Critics note that it might be possible for certain cultural patterns, such as fathers deserting mothers and children or unwillingness to defer gratification, to be passed on from generation to generation. But it is difficult for many to extend the culture of poverty to explain high rates of unemployment or underemployment, low income, a persistent shortage of cash, crowded living conditions, or homelessness.

Shaping our ideas.   Each of us receive numerous cultural messages every day which somehow support or contradict our particular interpretation of reality. When a problem such as homelessness appears, we normally look to our "cultural toolbox" to help us think about its causes. Often those ideas are transmitted to us from prominent individuals or groups who have the power to influence our lives. Critics often blame the Reagan administration for labelling homelessness as an insignificant problem for which the homeless themselves were probably to blame. These messages were often derived from the popular cultural themes that we have just discussed.

Profile:
Symbolically correct

Ronald Reagan's now classic insight about how homeless people "choose their own condition" is only the tip of the trash in the symbol-purveyor's dumpster. Other administration officials quickly jumped in to join him. HUD Secretary Samuel Pierce, Jr., claimed that seventy percent of the people on the streets "want to be there." Attorney General Edwin Meese claimed that people eat in soup kitchens "because it is cheap."

Have these public pronouncements encouraged anti-homeless attitudes? Robert Coates, the author of a recent book on the homeless, claims that some people have an interest in buttressing some of the myths that are helping to keep American homelessness in place. He says that "scurrilous articles are written for the purpose of underlining selected distortions and lies about the homeless" (Coates, p.200). Coates sites examples of newspaper editorials claiming that "the main problem of the homeless is that they are unsightly", and that the reason the problem exists is because the "liberals let them out of the loony bin." Coates claims that major sources are various conservative organizations who believe that money can be made through the manipulation of urban real estate. By undermining the efforts of community providers, their devalued property can be profitably redeveloped.

But incidental anti-homeless slurs can also be found. Respectable publications sometimes embellish, obscure, or entertain rather than objectively inform. For example, a major weekly newsmagazine described a new Los Angeles shelter as the only one a guest had ever seen with a "stereo in the bathroom." Newspaper reports have described local T-shirts with "eat the homeless" messages or with "troll busters" cartoons (a caricature of a drooling degenerate covered by a red circle and a slash). A recently opened full-service shelter in San Diego is commonly referred to as the Taj Mahal, and reporters, always on the lookout for new witticisms, like to use a new name sometimes given to shelters, "work-free drug places". On the other hand, an analysis of favorable articles would show that the typical homeless subjects profiled are often hard-luck families, or children, an atypical collection by any count. Even homeless advocate Robert Hayes complained about how often a congressional committee called and needed witnesses for a hearing - families, out of work in the past four months and white.

Whether any of this really changes peoples' minds about the homeless is debatable. But misrepresenting the homeless as mainstream citizens or as cave-dwelling trolls only polarize or confuses people. Some homeless providers have claimed that all of this has dulled the country's concern and has fed a backlash into the idea chain of workable solutions. As Mark Twain said, "It's not what people know that gets them in trouble, it's what they know that ain't so."

Is homelessness a product of the personal flaws of homeless individuals or is it the result of social conditions beyond the control of the individual? Our cultural ideas suggest that individualism and self-determination are very important and that anyone ought to be able to make it, especially if one works hard. Everyone is free to choose his or her own life, even if that choice means homelessness. Our culture also suggests that race and social class are still important qualities that contribute to our confusion about equal opportunity and welfare programs. While it is clear that certain cultural themes have influenced our opinions about homelessness, it is equally important to remember that the culture shapes the collective response of our policy makers when they attempt to confront the problem of homelessness. We might reasonably conclude that the particular cluster of cultural ideas that we have discussed has had the effect of consistently perpetuating the problem of homelessness in America beyond a timely solution. We will turn to this topic in the next chapter.

Chapter Four
The Causes of Homelessness

Our profile of homeless people in the introductory chapter featured Billy, a former mental patient, and John T., a crack cocaine user. Our profile also included the family of Lionel, Veralina, and their son. And it included Arch, who has been a working man all his life. Each of the ways that we describe these people contain significant cultural images that may be positive or negative. For example, we may be more sympathetic toward the plight of a young family headed by Lionel and Veralina than we would toward John T. because of his addiction. We might conclude that Arch has not been fairly treated, but we might feel that people like Billy should be arrested if they are hanging around a park bothering everyone.

What causes homelessness and what should we do about it? We have already seen how our cultural ideas influence the way in which people think about success and failure, opportunity and equality, work and responsibility. Cultural ideas will also influence how society collectively defines the causes of homelessness and responds by creating social policies directed to the problem. These policies, and the groups, organizations, and agencies that are created from them, will have an impact upon the lives of homeless people in countless ways. For example, if the causes of homelessness are attributed to individual flaws or qualities, then treatments, confinement, or motivational rhetoric may be emphasized as solutions. On the other hand, if changed social conditions such as recent chronic and massive unemployment or severe low-income housing shortages are seen as the primary causes, then policies that stress supplementing income or providing housing subsidies will be emphasized as solutions. In this chapter we will examine the various ways that policy makers have defined the causes of homelessness, and the subsequent solutions that have been implemented.

Homelessness, as we know it today, is largely a recent phenomenon. You may be able to sense this recency by counting the number of references in print in the 1970s and comparing it with the 1980s or the 1990s. This relatively sudden appearance of homelessness in the U.S. was met by the relative lack of comprehensive or satisfactory explanations. Early responses by officials were sometimes influenced by traditional cultural labels that focused upon the personal flaws of individuals.

Homelessness as a legal problem. A wide variety of legal procedures have enabled authorities to respond to the significant increases in homelessness in cities. For years, various public nuisance laws have been utilized to keep the city streets free from those who would likely offend others. These laws included vagrancy (or the lack of evidence of an officially-recognized address), loitering, panhandling, urinating or defecating in public, and other highly-specific violations such as rummaging through garbage dumpsters (which constitute private property). The solution to the problem was a jail sentence, or as ethnographer James Spradley recounted, "time in the bucket." Spradley, who, during the 1960s, spent years tracking and interviewing tramps (a self-defined identity among marginally homeless men), discovered an incredibly complex and sometimes symbiotic relationship between public needs and homeless people.

"If a man hasn't made the bucket, he isn't a tramp," Spradley's informants would often reply. Of a group of more than two hundred men asked to estimate the number of times they had been in jail, most responses were "over fifty" or "about a hundred times." Spradley estimated that for some of these men, much of their adult lives had been lived as inmates in local jails. In fact, Spradley identified "buckets" as one of the five major places where these men spent their lives.

Of course, arresting and jailing a person will instantly solve a homeless problem. But it will also solve, according to Spradley, some city employment needs. While attempting to discover the various identities common to these men, Spradley asked what kinds of inmates became "trusties," or helpers, in the jail.

It was discovered that there were about sixty categories of trusties! Those who

become trusties in the Seattle city jail work
at an enormous number of jobs: they staple
targets, mow lawns, mop floors, change
tires, wash cars, clean boats, clean toilets,
make coffee, usher in the court, care for the
sick, press clothes, make pastries, wait on
bulls (guards), carry messages, wash pots,
run elevators, cut hair, and a variety of
other tasks, In this jail, which has a
capacity for approximately 500 inmates,
nearly 150 trusties are required each day to
work. It was estimated by one police official
that 80 percent of the inmates at any time
are those charged with public drunkenness
and these are the men chosen to become
trusties because their crimes are not serious
nor is there much difficulty if they escape
(Spradley, p.84).

Although these men would readily seek trusty
positions because it would make their sentence
more bearable, there was a widespread feeling
that they were sometimes arrested because
trusties were needed. This perception of being
used to work in the jail was shared by police and
court officials (Spradley, p.85).

Jailing as a solution to homelessness began to lose
favor with cities when restraints were imposed
upon criminal justice systems, and when it was
discovered that far too much police time was taken
up by these arrest practices. However, many
cities are still struggling with the public legalities
associated with homelessness. Ongoing disputes

have regularly occurred between city officials and legal advocates regarding whether the homeless have residency rights in public areas. Officials are frustrated by the presence of numerous undesirables congregating in popular public areas such as subway stations or libraries or permanently camped in parks or plazas across from the mayor's office. Protections against selective arrest are constantly weighed against the notions of what constitutes a public nuisance or simply unattractive appearance. Typical legal labels conferred upon homeless people include "vagrant," "public nuisance," or even "criminal."

Many cities derive significant income from tourism and the sight of such a collection of people may offend the convention trade. An extreme example of this was a dispersal policy practiced in Phoenix in the early 1980s. It was felt that if the city provided no facilities or services, then the homeless would all leave. Numerous ordinances were passed including making it illegal to scavenge for recyclable material in dumpsters, while the city attempted to close down through zoning and other means most of the food programs and shelters. In other cities, "street sweeps" are often conducted by police who may offer referrals to shelters or missions as an alternative to arrest. A very controversial case occurred in New York City in 1987 when a woman refused to leave her sidewalk claim, and was arrested and temporarily confined against her will in a psychiatric hospital. A court ordered her release and she returned to her sidewalk.

Homelessness, as a social problem, cannot be resolved by these kinds of legal tactics. Most homeless people are not a public nuisance, nor do they deserve to be treated like criminals. Clearly public-use problems exist, but to connect these with the issue of homelessness detracts from any discussion of the real causes.

Homelessness as a medical condition.

Sometimes closely associated with the legal model is a *medical model*. According to this view, homeless people are victims of some kind of medical condition or disease and thus should be treated. In this view, they become either victims or patients, and it is likely that their status might be somewhat improved. To be a patient, though, still suggests a dependent status, one in which various rights are abridged, and where some common freedoms are restricted. The two most common medical statuses or labels attached to homeless persons are *addict* and *mentally ill*.

The labels "drunk" or "alcoholic" offered a convenient and plausible explanation for why someone would abandon a home and live in wretched surroundings. This status, which was voluntarily adopted according to the traditional public view, was in some ways less desirable than the status of jail inmate. Stories and images of drunks harassing people in the streets, sleeping in alleys and dumpsters, falling down in front of traffic, and wandering into fancy department stores demanding to use the bathroom filled the popular imagination. When the American Medical

Association announced in 1956 that alcoholism should be recognized as a disease, cities began to redefine their practice of treating street drunks as common criminals. But as the arrest procedures became more humane, including cushioning paddy wagons and providing rubberized floors and benches in cells, funding became increasingly scarce. No money was made available to establish a massive civil detoxification and alcoholic services network to serve as an alternative to the old ways. Today, researchers agree that alcohol is a significant problem for some homeless people. Alcohol abuse is difficult to measure and it is hard to determine if it led to someone's homelessness. It is probable that about one-third of the homeless population have some kind of problem with alcohol, a rate about two to three times higher than that of the population of the U.S. as a whole. This rate has remained relatively constant over the years.

The label "drug addict" also conveys a reasonable explanation for why someone would become homeless. Evidence of drug abuse among homeless people is generally hard to interpret since many studies have focused on populations other than the homeless. It is likely, though, that the increases of serious drug abuse, particularly of crack cocaine, in recent years have had a devastating effect on some people and increased their likelihood of becoming homeless. Estimates of drug abuse among the homeless range from about ten to twenty five percent (Burt, pp.115-116). Recent increases in drug use may also help to explain why the homeless population did not decline in the last few years although it is likely that the percentage of homeless persons with drug abuse problems has remained about the same for many years. It is also likely that increases in both alcohol and drug abuse among the general population has resulted in more homeless people with these problems than has been the case since the Great Depression (Burt, p.120).

Many people also associate homelessness with *mental illness*. Certainly, anyone would have to be "crazy" to live wandering the streets during the day and sleeping in the weeds at night. As we recall from Chapter 2, this kind of labelling of the homeless has been common throughout history. But contemporary analysis of homelessness includes considerable discussion of the role of mental illness. Are homeless people mentally ill and is it the cause of homelessness?

Many years ago, mental institutions (or "insane asylums," as they used to be called) operated with meager funds in perhaps the most ancient of public buildings. In 1955, the population of state hospitals for the mentally ill was about 550,000; today the population stands at about 100,000. Over the years, many of these patients were released, a process that is referred to as the *deinstitutionalization* of the mentally ill. In addition, many mental institutions were closed and the total number of available beds was reduced accordingly. Actually, the process of deinstitutionalization began in the 1940s, but most discussion of this topic centers around events that occurred in the 1960s and 1970s.

Three important factors led to increasing releases of patients. First, *psychotropic* or mood-altering drugs became increasingly popular among health practitioners, made patients easier to handle and increased their chances of being released. Second, community-based treatment programs became increasingly popular with psychologists and other practitioners as part of an efficiency-based and modernizing movement directed at what were considered medieval institutions. Third, legal decisions made it increasingly difficult to institutionalize people without their consent or to subject them to treatments for very long. People could be temporarily confined in emergencies, but for any long-term treatment a hearing would have to be held, a patient would have to agree, and "the least restrictive environment" for treatment would have to be determined.

How did these changes in institutionalization and treatment work? Many behavioral scientists feel that these so-called improvements resulted in serious problems. According to research psychiatrist E. Fuller Torrey, "the fiscal organization of public psychiatric services in the United States is more thought-disordered than most of their patients" (Torrey, p.35). Torrey claims that the intent is to discharge patients as quickly as possible, without concern about where they receive further treatment or whether they become homeless. In addition, funding and programs have never fully met the anticipated needs of newly-released patients. Community-based outpatient care was not designed to replace the total care of an institution, and the result is a labyrinth of overlapping and sometimes competing programs and services that can not adequately meet the total needs of patients. In addition, many of the drugs thought to be cures produced unpleasant aftereffects or were simply not used regularly in a non-supervised community environment. Also, the movement to protect the rights of the mentally ill has been highly controversial. Laws originally drafted to respond to a sometimes cruel system that tended to keep people imprisoned in insane asylums, became in the name of civil liberties, the means to sentence mentally incompetent people to a life of misery in the streets (DiIulio, p.35).

What kind of effect did deinstitutionalization have upon homelessness? The opinions of experts are divided. Clearly, most deinstitutionalization occurred in the 1960s, and by the late 1970s most of the people destined to be released already were. Now a decade or more later, it is questionable how many homeless people are a direct product of deinstitutionalization. But the changed concepts of public treatment may have had an effect that essentially duplicate the past numbers of mentally ill who happened to be homeless. For example, Rael Isaac and Virginia Armat, authors of *Madness in the Streets*, claim that deinstitutionalization contributed a great deal to the current problems of homelessness. They feel that additional victims of deinstitutionalization are to be found among the uninstitutionalized homeless people on the street. The predecessors of these chronically mentally ill young people would have gone to state mental hospitals that today will not treat them. And Torrey notes that given the forty-one percent increase in the nation's population since 1955, there would be some 800,000 people in mental institutions today, if there was no deinstitutionalization. He also notes that studies indicate that approximately one-third of recently discharged patients of state hospitals become at least intermittently homeless within six months of release. Given that far fewer people are institutionalized at all today, it would seem reasonable to believe estimates that approximately one-third of homeless people either have been or are now victims of mental illness (Torrey, p.35).

In general, it may be argued that medical conditions are related to homelessness. Homeless people report poorer health than comparable non-homeless populations, are often substance abusers, and suffer from mental illness. However, it is also important to realize that some people will use these conditions as political labels that suggest personal fault or blame. For example, former Secretary of Health and Human Services Margaret Heckler stated

> The problem of homelessness is not a new problem. It is correlated to the problem of alcohol or drug dependency. And there have been a number of alcoholics who become

homeless throughout the years, maybe centuries. They are still there... I see the mentally handicapped as the latest group of the homeless. But, the problem is as old as time and with this new dimension complicating it, it's a serious problem, but it always has been (Hopper and Hamberg, p.33).

Although the emotional tug is powerful, labelling homeless people in this way does not recognize numerous other homeless categories that include children, families, and working people. Also, it is not clear whether these medical problems are the cause or the result of being homeless.

Homeless people are likely to receive poorer quality health care than others, and are likely to be subject to a greater risk of disease due to their surroundings. Whether one drinks or uses drugs excessively may be as much a result of being homeless as the original cause of it. Finally, mental illness comes in many varieties which would include those forms developed from living on the streets. Thus, the medical model is useful in defining contributing factors that might place someone at high risk of becoming homeless. But to conclude that it is a primary cause of homelessness would be debatable.

Homelessness as a family problem. Another way of attempting to understand the causes of homelessness is to use a *family model* approach. Many people would likely conclude that homelessness is a result of family problems, suggesting individuals who are unable to get along with others or who suffer from the conditions previously described. Others might conclude that homelessness is the result of a breakdown of the family suggesting long-term social trends. Many people are also likely to think of a typical family as a married couple with two children and the husband as wage earner, as television programs portrayed many years ago. However, that family arrangement is not so typical anymore. In fact, less than ten percent of all families today fit that description and one parent households are more common today than the typical family described above.

These changes in the structure of the family have been shaped by the Industrial Revolution. Agricultural families, many years ago, required many members for mutual support and for labor. Since the *extended family,* or a family that includes other relatives and generations, is primarily an economic unit, family members became obligated to each other. This was particularly true in times and places where few social or welfare services were available. As our society industrialized, people moved to cities and began to live in smaller family groups. The *nuclear family,* or a family of parents and children, does not resemble its predecessor. These families have lower birth rates, grant greater freedoms to individual family members, and allow other people and groups to perform many family functions. For example, schools now assume responsibility for education, and governments assume more responsibility for assistance to those in need. Also, industrial work separated family members from each other for much of the day at the same time that members became increasingly dependent upon each other for mutual affection and personal rewards. The strains derived from choosing a mate primarily for love and expecting emotional support for more than five decades has resulted in a high rate of divorce and the development of alternative family structures.

Have changes in the family structure contributed to homelessness? One of the striking features of the new homeless that began to be recognized in the early 1980s was the increase of families finding themselves without shelter. Two principal factors seem to have contributed to an increasing number of families becoming homeless - changes in divorce laws and disintegration of family ties.

In the 1970s divorce laws in the United States were revised and a no-fault process was established to dissolve marriages without blame and to divide property more equally. But subsequent studies, indicated that women, especially exclusive homemakers, suffered under these new arrangements. Ex-husbands' standards of living typically rose by forty-two percent and ex-wives' dropped by seventy-three percent after divorce. Since the vast majority of women did not receive alimony and fewer than half received child support payments, the rate of personal disaster and subsequent homelessness for women rose accordingly (Weitzman, 1985).

As previously discussed, *social isolation* is a common characteristic of the homeless. The homeless "are decidedly different from other poor persons in at least one significant respect: they are profoundly alone" (King, p.32). Homeless people who have family connections may find a partial source of support through temporary housing or financial gifts and loans. However, it is possible that the generosity or resources of these people will eventually run out. But most homeless people - some fifty-seven percent - have never married. Many others are divorced or separated. The remaining few that are still with families are typically women with dependent children. In general, many homeless people have minimal contact with family or relatives or do not wish to return to the family. This is particularly true with regard to young homeless women who have experienced previously troublesome family situations. With weak or nonexistent ties to others, homeless people are "especially vulnerable to the vagaries of fortune occasioned by changes in employment, income, or physical or mental heath" (Rossi and Wright, p.138).

How has the recent rise of homelessness been influenced by changes in the family structure that occurred decades ago? The United States experienced a tremendous increase in its urban population during this century. For example, about forty-four percent of the population in 1940 lived in rural areas, compared to only twenty-seven percent today. A typically aged thirty-five-year-old homeless person would have been raised by parents who were about as likely to have come from urban areas as rural. Many homeless people may have at one time experienced strong rural, extended family ties that seriously deteriorated in their own lifetime, due to urban migration. Many homeless people were also members of first generation urban nuclear families with little historical guidance for living this way. Therefore, if homelessness is a family problem, it could be defined as a consequence of a deteriorating or absent family structure significantly influenced by recent social trends. But is it possible that these conditions and others previously discussed somehow escape the heart of the homelessness problem?

The definition of homelessness as a lack of permanent shelter would imply that provision of housing would be a logical solution. Obviously, the lack of available, acceptable, and affordable long-term, permanent shelter suitable to become a home is the result of many complex social forces. Two significant processes have contributed to our housing-related problems of homelessness: providing ways for people to earn enough money to afford housing, and the nature and extent of the nation's housing inventory.

Homelessness in a post-industrial society.
More than one hundred years ago, the process of industrialization brought about revolutionary changes in the ways that cities functioned and

76

what people did in their daily lives. As factories were built, the need for labor increased and city populations grew dramatically. After World War II, the United States experienced another revolution and became what might be called a *post-industrial* society. Again, people's daily lives were changed. Just as agricultural employment changed to manufacturing during the Industrial Revolution, a post-industrial society experiences a decline in manufacturing and an increase in services. "Service occupations" are a very broad category today, and include such jobs as lawyer, maid, pizza deliveryperson, and even the President of the United States. Approximately ninety percent of all jobs added since 1970 were in the service sector. Today more than seventy percent of all employed people work in service sector occupations.

What impact has this changing of jobs had upon cities and homelessness? During the last two decades the global economy has grown as more and more manufacturing centers relocated in less developed parts of the world and employed workers at lower wages. It is also true that many other factories and business have relocated to the suburbs or what used to be rural areas. Many *deindustrialized* American cities have not recovered from the loss of these jobs and the abandonment of factories and businesses. As factories closed, cities lost tax revenues, and stores went out of business. It has been estimated that there were over two million abandoned buildings in central cities nationwide by 1977 (Spates,

PRICE AND INFLATION

PURCHASING POWER OF THE DOLLAR

YEAR	PRICE
1970	2.574
1980	1.215
1990	0.766

A 1982 Dollar would have bought $2.57 worth of merchandise in 1970. In 1990 only $0.76 of merchandise could be purchased with the same dollar. (Source: U.S. Bureau of Labor Statistics)

CONSUMER PRICE INDEX

YEAR	CPI
1970	38.8
1980	82.4
1990	130.7

The "cost of living" index measures the average change in prices relative to a base year (1983) of 100. (Source: U.S. Bureau of the Census, Current Reports) p.372).   Many cities attempted to improve job opportunities by revitalizing their downtown areas with new office buildings, convention centers andeven festival marketplaces, but these attempts, sometimes called "pockets of plenty" in languishing city centers, rarely had an impact upon real job needs. According to Bennett Harrison and Barry Bluestone, who examined the recent corporate restructuring of America, the majority of jobs created since the 1970s have offered poverty level wages. Service-type jobs usually offer limited opportunities for workers to move up a career ladder, a reason why many are referred to as dead-end jobs. In addition, the minimum wage and welfare benefits have fallen far behind the rate of inflation. Clearly, more and more poor people are finding it increasingly difficult to maintain a satisfactory employment pattern.

> Not surprisingly, more and more of America's homeless are families with children and people with jobs. A survey released in December 1990 by the U.S. Conference of Mayors found that almost one-quarter of the homeless work, but have wages too low to afford permanent housing. Apart from those who live on the streets or in shelters, there are millions more who live doubled or tripled-up in overcrowded apartments, and millions of others who pay more than they can reasonably afford for substandard housing. As a result of this situation, millions of low-income Americans

are only one rent increase, one hospital stay, one layoff away from becoming homeless (Dreier and Appelbaum, p.48).

Inequality, or the difference between wealth and poverty, has increased since the 1970s. Generally, in the 1970s and the 1980s the rich got richer from higher earnings. In the 1980s the poor got poorer from lower earnings. Therefore, poor people have realized increasingly limited amounts of money available for rent. Also, deindustrialization contributed to a shortage of the traditional kinds of jobs available for poor people. Many workers who became unemployed during the high unemployment times of the early 1980s were unable to find suitable work in later years due to the decrease of lower skill level opportunities. Unemployment is a likely first step toward homelessness and long-term unemployment significantly decreases one's likelihood to become permanently employed again. In addition, it was much harder during the 1980s for poor people to get out of poverty even if they worked. In 1987, approximately two-thirds of the working poor had incomes of $167 a week, which would not raise them above the poverty line (Burt, p.73). If income is based upon an hourly wage of $4.35, a family wage earner would have to work more than sixty-one hours a week to rise above the poverty line for a family of four. According to a survey by the Urban Institute in 1987, homeless single men reported a typical income of $143 a month. Single women reported an income of $183 a month, and homeless women with children reported a typical monthly income of $300 (Burt, pp.55-56). Median rentals in all major cities are typically hundreds of dollars higher. Since there was also a loss of more than a million cheaper rental units during the previous decade, it is even harder for poor people to locate a suitable residence. In addition, beginning in the 1980s, renters faced increased financial pressures in other facets of their lives, which left a smaller proportion of their income available for rent. This *rent burden*, or the percent of the family budget necessary to pay rent, increased by twenty-five percent in most areas of the country during the 1970 - 1988 period. The result is that most poor people will pay rent beyond a commonly recommended thirty percent of their income. In 1985, four out of five poor renter households paid more than thirty-five percent of their income for rent. Even more dramatic, more than half of these same households paid more than sixty percent of their income for rent (Burt, p.45).

Homelessness as an affordable housing problem. If it is true that deindustrialization has reduced people's ability to pay rent, then has the housing market responded accordingly to make housing more affordable? According to Martha Burt, a researcher for the Urban Institute, the number of rental units in the last decade has been consistently inadequate to meet needs. Yet the housing benefit programs of the 1970s served more people, were worth more, and were less punitive than during the 1980s. But in the 1980s changes in the tax codes, housing price inflation, and high interest rates changed the rental housing market (Burt, p.63).   All of these factors had an impact on the number of rental units available for the homeless and their affordabilty. Since the housing industry has been traditionally dominated by small, private sector builders, this leaves the government as the only entity capable of truly influencing or regulating any aspect of housing. Federal approaches dealing with the housing-related problems of homelessness began in the 1930s and have included building *public housing* directly for the poor primarily in the 1950s, *subsidizing private developers'* efforts to build low-income housing after the 1960s, and offering *income assistance* to individuals for housing after the mid-1970s.

The Federal government began to build public housing primarily as an emergency measure during the Great Depression. Under the Housing Act of 1937, the federal government supplied funds to *local housing authorities*, a type of government agency, that built and managed public housing projects. About 500,000 units were built by the mid-1950s. A similar number was built beginning in the late 1960s, but, beginning in the 1980s, new construction dropped considerably. Increased costs of building, neighborhood opposition, private real estate and developer opposition, some highly publicized failures and scandals, and the lack of government funding led to a decline of new construction. The result was an "absolute shortage in appropriate rental units to accommodate poorly housed families" (Burt, p.33).

Public housing projects, once designed for temporary usage by a mixed group of low-income people, have, in recent years, become the housing of last resort by the very poorest people who have little, if any, choice.

Revitalization of housing has occurred, but often for a group distinctly different from the homeless. The term *gentrification* is derived from the practice of renovating run-down nineteenth-century London homes by the wealthy landed gentry or members of the ruling class. Today, it refers to the movement of relatively affluent people into older, declining neighborhoods, and to renovating housing often more for economic potential than for immediate housing needs. People are likely to move to the city and gentrify for a number of reasons, including the cultural attractions of city life, changes in family composition, proximity to employment in revitalized areas, and potential bargains. Critics of gentrification claim that it almost always displaces the previous poorer inhabitants by causing taxes and rents to rise.

> As the affluent and the poor began to compete for scarce inner-city housing, prices skyrocketed. Low-rent apartments were converted to high-priced condominiums. Rooming houses, the last refuge of the poor, were torn down or turned into upscale apartments. Businesses catering to the poor and working class families were replaced by high-priced shops and restaurants (Dreier

and Appelbaum, p.48).

Researchers estimate that newly gentrified houses have contributed to the disappearance of some thirty percent of low-income housing units in recent history.

Profile:
New York City, Home of the Homeless

Homelessness is visible and common in the nation's largest city. Estimates for the total number of homeless range from about 30,000 to more than 100,000 in a city of some 7,000,000. Every day, homeless people attempt to contract for city services and benefits, but just as often they seem to be huddled in doorways and subway stations from Central Park to Coney Island. About 25,000 people sleep in cots in the city operated shelters, the only system of its kind in the U.S. Other cities contract with private non-profit groups to provide shelter. The $500,000,000 program funds facilities like the seven-hundred bed Fort Washington Armory, located in an upper Manhattan region that few other New Yorkers would care to visit. It costs the city about $18,000 per person each year to maintain its shelters and provide their numerous services. This translates to approximately $1500 per month in a city where a few years ago, many homeless people typically stayed in single room occupancies (SRO's) for less than $100 a week. But during the urban revitalization days of the 1980s, many SRO's were demolished eliminating some 80,000 beds.

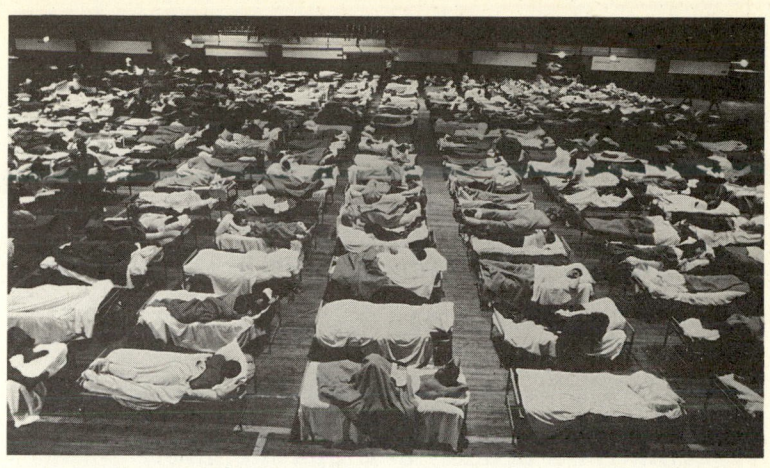

Fort Washington Armory

According to recent studies, the majority of single adults in city shelters are drug users and ex- convicts, although typical residents are usually peaceful men down on their luck. Nevertheless, shelters are a world by themselves and violent incidents are a daily affair. About 13,000 homeless New Yorkers are mentally ill and 30,000 are HIV- positive or have AIDS. Recently enacted city policies prohibit anyone from sleeping in bus and subway stations, even when temperatures fall below freezing. Plans to build additional smaller shelters have resulted in frequent "not in my backyard" protests. Meanwhile, the Housing Authority is pursuing other plans to allow low-income people to buy their apartments in new public housing projects.

In the last twenty years a typical family's expenditure on a new mortgage increased from twenty-five percent to fifty percent of their income. As fewer people are able to afford new housing, older housing becomes more attractive for gentrification. And, as rents have increased, what is ordinarily seen as acceptable housing continues to be redefined downward. Today,

> some eighty-five percent of low-income renters are paying at least 30 percent of their income for housing. Two-thirds of the poor are paying at least half of their income just for housing. The typical young single mother pays over seventy percent of her meager income just to keep a room over her children's heads. Perhaps the most important statistic is this: Only one-quarter of poor households receive any kind of housing subsidy - the lowest level of any industrial nation in the world. The swelling waiting lists for even the most deteriorated subsidized housing projects are telling evidence of the desperation of the poor in the private housing market (Dreier and Appelbaum, p.47).

Like Monopoly, the search for decent housing has become a game with the homeless seeking housing of last resort; many are destined to lose. For most of us, housing is the result of a private agreement between an owner and a tenant or buyer. We shop around, assess the area, the amenities, and the costs. As we make our choices in this free-market system, the least desirable housing supposedly "trickles down" and becomes available for the lowest income groups. Unfortunately for many homeless people, this theory does not work. Studies indicate that there is often a serious

HOUSING AFFORDABILITY

AFDC AVERAGE MONTHLY BENEFITS, 1990

FAMILY	$389
INDIVIDUAL	$135

MONTHLY EARNINGS, 1990

ALL WORKERS, average.	$1384
POVERTY: (1 person)*	$524
POVERTY: (3 persons)*	$880
MINIMUM WAGE**	$680

*Poverty line maximum earnings per family size
** Earnings at $4.25 for a 40-hour week.

FAIR MARKET RENTS FOR SELECTED METROPOLITAN AREAS, 1991

AREA	1 BEDROOM	2 BEDROOM
Boston, MA	$739	$869
Chicago, IL	$543	$635
Houston, TX	$364	$429
Los Angeles, CA	$642	$747
New York, NY	$531	$625
San Francisco, CA	$775	$919
Seattle, WA	$507	$592
Washington, DC	$621	$731

Source: The Universal Almanac, 1992

mismatch between the supply of available housing and the actual needs of various low-income groups. For example, many people attempt to obtain housing using the federal government's assistance programs. Yet, over one-half of all those qualified recipients are unable to find acceptable housing within the allotted time period of two months (Burt, p.43).

Although there are approximately 3.3 million low-income housing units in the United States today, they must serve a poverty population of approximately 35.7 million people. Approximately 4.6 million households receive rental subsidies. No other major industrial nation has such a lack of acceptable housing or such a problem with homelessness. At no time since the Great Depression have housing needs been so critical.

Homelessness: compiling the causes. The election of Ronald Reagan as president in 1979 marked a significant change not only in attitudes toward the homeless, but also in many governmental programs and missions. Reagan, in 1984, said,

> One problem we've had, even in the best of times is the people who are sleeping on the grates, the homeless who are homeless, you might say, by choice (New York Times, p.A24).

The policies of the Reagan administration contributed to what was already becoming a growing national crisis. A common pattern of blaming the victim by attributing homelessness to poor choice or other personal characteristics such as drunkenness or mental illness characterized the comments made by members of his administration. It is not surprising, then, that new national policies had a negative impact upon the poor and the homeless. For example,

> Housing shouldered the largest burden of the Reagan budget axe. Since 1981, federal housing assistance has been slashed from about $33 billion to less than $8 billion a year. The number of new federally subsidized apartments built each year dwindled from over 200,000 in the 1970s to less than 15,000 last year. To put this in perspective, in 1981, the federal government was spending seven dollars for defense for every one dollar that is spent on housing. By 1989, it spent over forty dollars on defense for every housing dollar (Dreier and Appelbaum, p.49).

Dreier and Appelbaum maintain that some subsidies actually did increase, but these mostly went to the fifteen percent of taxpayers that make over $50,000 year. On the other hand, federal housing officials during the Bush presidency maintained that housing assistance spending rose every year during the 1980s. They claimed that affordable housing was more likely lost as a result of urban renewal, inflation, speculation, and tax policy than any supposed federal budget cuts.

89

Excessive regulation has also been mentioned as a reason for housing affordability problems. According to this view, regulations including land-use controls, restrictive building codes, growth and rent controls have driven developers out of residential housing markets. Proponents of this position cite the case of Houston as "a growth-happy community with no zoning and rental vacancies of 18 percent." (Tucker, p.27) In general, the national housing crisis is defined as a local problem.

Housing was not the only program that was cut back by the Reagan administration. Other programs that give assistance to the homeless suffered similar fates. For example, cuts in Aid to Families with Dependent Children resulted in hundreds of thousands of qualified families becoming disqualified. In addition, billions of dollars were cut from food stamp and health care programs. Meanwhile, the Department of Housing and Urban Development claimed that the total number of homeless people in 1984 was only about 250,000-350,000, an estimate dramatically lower than estimates made by practitioners and advocates of the time.

The efforts to minimize the problem of homelessness and to cut assistance was part of a strategy that claimed that homelessness was largely a local problem and was mostly the result of personal pathologies. But personal pathologies probably cause homelessness far less often than those factors or conditions that are beyond an individual's control. For example, it may seem at first that various legal, medical or family problems have their roots in poor choices made by individuals. Someone chooses to become an addict or does not try to make a marriage work and the eventual consequence is homelessness. But a more critical examination will reveal that choices are always made in a greater environmental context that may be quite different from our own lives. The temptation to blame the victim is a prejudicial attitude that is supported by some very powerful cultural ideas that may tell us more about ourselves than the problem that we are supposedly examining. On the other hand, precipitating economic and political conditions including recent impoverishment due to divorce, welfare cuts, unemployment and underemployment due to a changing economy, and the dramatic escalation of housing costs in most cities has more than likely caused the majority of homelessness today. These are conditions which have very little to do with personal choice.

So far, we have examined how various cultural factors have shaped our collective ideas regarding the causes and the solutions to homelessness. We have also seen that the problem of homelessness has not been resolved when these cultural explanations focus heavily upon personal flaws instead of concentrating on more complex societal causes. In fact, by cutting assistance programs the seriousness of homelessness as a problem has increased and has become more difficult to solve. Is there any way to resolve this problem and what

are some of the possible solutions? We will turn to
this topic in the next chapter.

Homeless in New York City

Chapter Five
Homelessness: Policies and Prospects

What kind of future is there for the ten homeless people profiled at the beginning of this book? Can Frank and Billy look forward to better treatment for their personal troubles? Will Sheila and her daughter stand a better chance of finding a suitable home with her Section 8 certificate? What are the chances that Lionel or Veralina will find a permanent job with sufficient income to house them and their son in something better than a tent?

So far, we have counted the homeless and discovered where they spend their lives. We have gained an understanding of the cultural forces that shape our ideas about why people are homeless. We have also reviewed the various causes of homelessness and the subsequent treatment of those affected. We now turn to the broader topic of *public policy*, those programs or procedures that determine the precise fate of individuals who attempt to contact officials when they are in need of help.

As we recall from the discussion on the history of homelessness, our first policies were local in nature. If any public responsibility was

determined, it was to provide minimal and
temporary help to locals who had exhausted all
other options for support. Subsidizing caretaker
families and providing space in local jails for the
homeless was a common pattern for most of our
history. Additional support became the
responsibility of private charities. Since a
common thread of personal responsibility for
success and failure has been characteristic of
American attitudes for most of our history, it is
not surprising that our public support programs
lagged behind those of other modern nations.
Most European nations had created extensive
"social safety nets" by the 1890s to protect citizens
from conditions beyond their control or to soften
the consequences of other detrimental life events.
The United States, however, waited until the
1930s to enact its first significant federal social
programs and it was not until the 1960s that
many social support programs reached a degree of
comprehensiveness to begin to rival that of other
modern nations. Even so, programs that were
implemented often resulted in placing the United
States in a second-rate position when compared to
the same programs in other nations. For example,
compared with other industrial nations, the
United States ranks at the bottom in the amount
of subsidized housing available to poor people.
Finally, the continuing legacy of popular attitudes
against the enactment of social support programs
has been very much in existence, due in part to
the fact that many people can actually remember
a time in America when someone would say
"nobody helped me - I had to do it myself." About

one- fifth of today's citizens were alive when there were no significant social support programs in existence, and half of today's citizens were born prior to the enactment of major social services programs in the 1960s.

What have been the most significant programs and policies that were developed in recent years? We may think of efforts to confront the problem of homelessness as falling into several categories: *advocacy approaches*, *government programs*, and *grass roots efforts*.

Advocacy for the homeless. Advocacy approaches to solve the problems of homelessness often involve *social movements*, or a non-official collective response to a social problem that people think can be solved. Groups of homeless people have staged protests, arranged demonstrations, organized marches, and camped in parks to draw attention to their plight or to advocate change. Various national or regional groups representing the homeless have attempted to establish local chapters and articulate homeless persons have become participants at public hearings.

Perhaps the most significant efforts to change public policy through popular advocacy were led by Mitch Snyder. Just before the 1984 election, Snyder began a fifty-one-day fast to draw attention to the nation's critical housing shortage. Specifically, he sought President Reagan's commitment to fund the renovation of a government-owned building in Washington D.C.

for use as a shelter. Eventually, in June of 1985, the President and Congress agreed to provide almost $5 million for the shelter. Snyder's numerous hunger strikes, campouts at places like Lafayette Square across the street from the White House, and appearances on various news programs helped focus national attention on the problem of homelessness during the 1980s. Snyder testified before Congressional subcommittees and was instrumental in the development of the first federal legislative program to help the homeless.

However, some observers feel that the efforts of reform groups have failed to gain even the most obvious emergency needs in any real or permanent way.

> Despite all the effort, even this most basic and least disputed goal has yet to be realized. Where shelter has been provided, moreover, its tendency has been to become not a waystation enroute to replacement quarters but a piece in what routinely appears as the puzzle of subsistence, to be solved by a variety of makeshifts (Caton, p.166).

Another advocacy tool has been *litigation*, including legal suits filed on behalf of the homeless or the resolution of court cases originating from arrests or citations. Early cases included the decriminalization of public drunkenness and challenges to the validity of arrests for a variety of "status" crimes, including vagrancy or loitering, on the grounds that they were virtually always applied to poor people on the streets. Other cases established the right of the homeless to receive shelter and to require that cities provide it. This was first granted in New York City in 1981 through the efforts of attorney and homeless advocate Robert Hayes. Hayes was concerned that only 3,000 beds were available for the estimated 30,000 homeless men, often in filthy buildings ravaged by crime and violence. He filed suit on behalf of six homeless men, and eventually, a constitutional responsibility to provide aid, care, and support for the needy was recognized by the court. New York City was then required to provide shelter to anyone who requested it.

Law suits have also been filed to challenge complicated bureaucratic procedures that are intended to help the homeless but may do the opposite. Early cases focused upon homeless people's lack of an address, an address being an often-imposed requirement for receiving any benefits. More recently, Los Angeles was required to modify its General Assistance procedures when it was claimed that many clients who had been late for caseworker appointments were denied assistance for up to sixty days as punishment. And in the same city it was charged that developmentally disabled indigent and homeless applicants for General Relief were effectively excluded because of an "exceedingly and unnecessarily complex and convoluted application process" (Ropers, p.193), which meant that they could not figure out how to get through the welfare bureaucracy.

Although advocacy approaches have been quite successful in resolving certain problems or at least producing a more tolerant attitude toward the homeless, a backlash in some cities has appeared. For example, sleeping in bus stations or camping in city parks is increasingly likely to violate new city ordinances. And some cities, including New York and Atlanta, have passed measures to restrict begging or aggressive panhandling. Cities also have experienced ongoing problems with rezoning ordinances or permits to build facilities for the homeless anywhere except for the slums.

Profile:
Homeless Advocates

Robert Hayes and Mitch Snyder, although differing in many respects, were both catalysts for change during the dreary days of homelessness in the early 1980s. Both helped to awaken Americans to the appalling conditions of homelessness and convinced them that something could be done.

Robert Hayes saw firsthand the plight of New York City's homeless and decided to do something about it. In 1979, the recent law school graduate sued the city and the state seeking adequate shelter for his six clients, including one whose residence was a cardboard box on Park Avenue. Even though it was his first court appearance and he was scared to death, he claimed that the state had a constitutional responsibility to provide shelter for anyone who requested it. The judge agreed and New York began to turn armories and other public buildings into shelters with cots, showers, and simple meals. Requests from other states led Hayes to quit his job with a top corporate law firm.and to form the National Coalition for the Homeless. Over the years, dozens of cities have learned from Hayes and the Coalition and have persuaded municipal officials and private organizations to pool their resources to help the homeless.

Mitch Snyder also left a well-paying job to take up the cause of the homeless. As passionate and zealous as Hayes was studious and methodical, Snyder typified the label of "activist" by being bothersome to many, particularly the Reagan administration. Losing sixty pounds during a fifty-one-day hunger strike, Snyder prodded President Reagan in 1984 to agree to fund an emergency shelter in Washington D.C. But one accomplishment simply led to another goal in Snyder's ongoing battle to "kick in doors where necessary" to help the homeless. Although a laudatory movie about him starring Martin Sheen made him famous, he continued to live in a shelter, and persistently challenged reluctant

Washington D.C. demonstration

authorities to act on his recommendations. He persuaded members of Congress to hold hearings at his Community for Creative Non-Violence shelter, and was instrumental in the creation of the McKinney Homeless Assistance Act of 1988.

Robert Hayes recently returned to his law practice. Mitch Snyder died in 1990.

Government Programs. Homeless people can rarely survive without help, but where should this help come from and what form should it take? As we recall, in earlier times, extended families mostly cared for those in need. But in more recent times, governments have assumed greater responsibility for helping the homeless.

Assistance by governments may take many forms, but basically falls into one of two categories: those programs that provide income, or cash assistance, and those programs that provide "income-in-kind," which may be goods or services. What types of income or income-in-kind policies and programs are provided for the homeless? The most important programs that make up the U.S. social safety net are Aid to Families with Dependent Children (AFDC), Supplemental Security Income (SSI), the Food Stamp Program, and General Assistance. In addition there are a variety of housing programs designed for low-income people. What are these programs and how have they helped the homeless?

Aid to Families with Dependent Children provides cash payments and allows a family to qualify for health care (Medicare) and food stamps. AFDC benefits have been slowly losing their value since the 1970s and have led to an increase in the risk of homelessness. Today, the average AFDC family receives some $180 less in real dollars than it did more than twenty years ago. In addition, after 1981 benefits regulations were changed, which resulted in some twenty-one percent of previously qualified persons either experiencing reductions or becoming ineligible for benefits. Studies indicate that a relatively low percentage, about one-third, of very needy families that the program was designed for actually received help from it. Furthermore, this money was insufficient to pay for housing and other expenses (Burt, p.86).

Supplemental Security Income provides additional income to poor aged, blind, or disabled persons who are prevented from working. Cash assistance can potentially give people nearly enough money to meet the poverty line, and since it is adjusted for purchasing power, the real dollars have remained stable. Studies indicate that very few mentally disabled people receive assistance for which they qualify. Also, in 1981 administrative procedures for eligibility become more strict and many disabled people were disqualified and lost their assistance until procedures were revised several years later. The largest share of SSI recipients are nonaged disabled persons, and in recent years there has been a greater effort to enroll qualified homeless people.

The Food Stamp Program allows poor people to buy, using coupons, nutritional food in grocery stores. Food stamps are intended to help poor people who attempt to improve their diet, although only about fifty-nine percent of poor people participate. The program also makes adjustments for those people whose rent burden is very high. Although the program has been adjusted for food costs at a modest level, those persons who have high rent burdens find it increasingly difficult to meet nutritional needs. This may indirectly contribute to the continued existence of some homelessness by allowing a better diet for those who remain in shelters. By escaping a high rent burden, they might possibly spend beyond the average per person benefit of about $59 per month.

Unemployment Insurance provides income to workers who have recently lost their jobs due to conditions beyond their control. This program will offer only temporary help, usually extending half a year, and usually will cover only about seventy-five to eighty percent of unemployed people. Few homeless people benefit from this program due to the nature of jobs commonly available to them.

General Assistance, sometimes known as public assistance or relief, is a local assistance effort that varies widely from place to place. Since there are no national standards, states or counties decide whether to offer it, who will qualify and for how long, and what kinds of help may be granted under what conditions. For example, one third of all states offer no General Assistance at all. For the homeless people who fall through the federal social safety net, even though they may actually qualify for one or more federal programs, the local relief programs are an essential last resort. But even this last resort will fail if it is not available in a certain state or county or if it excludes certain categories of people.

In general, homeless people often remain homeless in large part because they receive little from government programs, despite the fact that they are very needy. Single homeless people, a very large portion of all homeless individuals, do not qualify for AFDC. Few are elderly, and therefore do not qualify for SSI and other programs targeted for that group. Some homeless are physically or mentally disabled, but very few have actually received help. General Assistance is often not available at all, and where it is, it may carry various restrictions. It was the presence of these conditions and the cinsiderable efforts of homeless advocates that ultimately led to the passage of significant legislation to help homeless people.

The Stewart B. McKinney Homeless Assistance Act was enacted in 1987 and initially allocated $355 million to fund crisis programs and to explore long-term solutions to homelessness. An Interagency Council on the Homeless was created to oversee programs in various cities and states, including grants for emergency shelters, transitional housing, and rehabilitation programs. To participate in McKinney act programs

103

administered by HUD and the departments of Education and Labor, eligible cities must develop comprehensive homeless assistance plans. The plans must include an inventory of local homeless facilities and services and an action strategy explaining how federal funds will help. Cities are encouraged to develop specific programs for the homeless including alcohol and drug treatment, shelter services to meet the increasingly diverse population, employment assistance, and health care. Cities are also required to identify underutilized properties that may be suitable for homeless assistance. National competition for funds has resulted in many unique and responsive programs, and, so far more than $600 million has been granted. Thousands of homeless persons have been served by the Health Services for the Homeless Program and various other assistance programs administered by local governments or nonprofit organizations. Although yearly funding amounts are always subject to political debate, experts claim that these programs represent federal anti-poverty policy at its best (DiIulio, p.34).

Housing programs have been a part of the social safety net since the 1930s. Debates have generally revolved around who should provide housing, and how (or if) it should be subsidized to make it affordable for poor people.

Public housing, always controversial, was particularly in disfavor by presidents in recent years. Critics claim that the Reagan and Bush

Administrations cut funds for public housing eighty percent since 1980. Instead, government policies have provided subsidies for existing housing and have encouraged tenants to manage and buy their own units with federal grants. Many new procedures were enacted into law by the Cranston-Gonzales National Affordable Housing Act of 1990, which created HOPE, the Homeownership and Opportunity for People Everywhere program. HOPE was designed to make tenants the owners of public housing. Units could be sold to resident management corporations, or to tenant groups. Tenants would become owners but resale value would be limited to allow for the recapture of proceeds by HUD and the tenant group. However, since public housing has become the housing of last resort for many very poor people today who are often unemployed, it will probably be of little use to most residents. Meanwhile, critics claim that these plans are an effort to sell off public housing and absolve the federal government of any further responsibility in this area.

Another program authorized by the Cranston-Gonzales legislation is the HOME Investment Partnerships Act. The HOME program will let cities decide what, where, how, and when to provide much needed housing assistance. Block grants may be used to provide incentives to develop and support affordable rental housing and home ownership programs. The program requires that at least thirty percent of the grant recipients must use funds for new construction, to counter a position that previous administrations have opposed. However, using funds for public housing operating subsidies or modernization is prohibited.

If more housing is built or rehabilitated, will it be affordable? A simple answer may be misleading. Rather, housing must be in the right place at the right time and appropriate for the potential renters who must be able to afford it. Simply counting the total number of affordable rentals in a city may not reveal the true need. Also, some experts do not believe that it is possible to profitably build or rehabilitate housing that poor people can afford. If that is true, then subsidizing rents and/or construction becomes a necessity.

Today, federal housing subsidies reach only about one-fourth of all poor households. Some of these subsidies are directed toward new construction projects or rehabilitation. Other subsidies are made available for renters who must choose from the existing private housing inventory in a city. Qualified recipients receive Section 8 rental certificates and landlords agree to rent according to federal government determined "fair market rents" typical for the locality. The federal government pays the landlord the difference between thirty percent of the tenant's income and the fair market rent. Section 8 *vouchers* are housing certificates that can be used anywhere. Applications are taken locally and waiting periods are often months and sometimes a year or more. In recent years, the number of poor households increased at the same time that rentals increased, so that fewer qualified poor people received subsidies. Also, single adults, the largest category of all homeless, have been effectively excluded from receiving subsidies.

All of these federal programs are funded differently depending upon legislative actions or the political party in power. Estimates of the extent of help granted to low-income families indicate that a greater proportion of all poor people were beneficiaries in the last few years than in the late 1970s. If greater help was granted, then why would there be an increase in homelessness? Experts suggest that benefits have not been proportionally divided, leaving some groups like the elderly and households with children receiving more benefits than others. In addition, regulatory changes, such as the amount of monetary deductions poor people can claim in calculating their housing subsidy qualifications, may have left a greater proportion of poor families at risk of becoming homeless. Finally, some states offer supplementary housing assistance to poor people and other states do not (Burt, p.96).

In general, social programs for poor people suffered serious setbacks during the last two decades. Several programs, such as AFDC, have lost their purchasing power, and others, such as General Assistance, have seen changes in regulations that diminished their services. Programs have always largely excluded single adults, the most sizable group of homeless. Housing availability is more difficult to determine.

Although the number of low-cost units declined, subsidies may have allowed more units to become affordable.   Clearly, the recent passage of new housing-related legislation such as the McKinney Act and the Cranston-Gonzales Act and the strong likelihood of increased appropriations by a supportive Congress and administration will be helpful to the homeless.

Grass roots efforts. Public and private agencies have often worked together to deal with the homeless and their needs. What has been the traditional role of private agencies and what is their role today? By definition, private groups define for themselves what role they wish to play and thus are not likely to feel as restricted as comparable public agencies in offering their services. In order to qualify as a tax-exempt organization helping the homeless, a group must be truly charitable and not use a substantial part of their resources for influencing legislation. In years past, organizations such as the YMCA and the Salvation Army have been active in helping local poor people with temporary shelter and other needs. In fact, at various times in American history, the idea of helping the homeless was synonymous with private charitable organizations.

Mostly, the present effort of the grass roots private sector has been a struggle to meet the demands of homeless people who seek shelter in church basements or line up for meals at soup kitchens. In 1983, the *Emergency Jobs Appropriations Act* established a major working relationship between private and public groups as the federal government sought to provide immediate winter needs in various cities across the nation. A National Board was established and included representatives from the United Way of America, the Salvation Army, the American Red Cross, the National Council of Churches of Christ in the USA, the National Conference of Catholic Charities, and the Council of Jewish Federations. The intent of the legislation was to allow local groups to become instrumental in formulating and providing assistance in their own areas. Studies have indicated that the efforts to raise funds and keep records has been extremely time consuming, although a number of exemplary programs have been identified (Cooper, p.136). Yet the overall impact of such programs is minimal. According to the president of the Robert Wood Johnson Foundation, a major contributor to homeless programs:

> We believe that our program shows that groups can come together and that something can be done. But we also know that it is a drop in the bucket. It cannot even pretend to solve the problems of the homeless in any big city - nor can any private initiative alone. The resources available from philanthropy, churches, and voluntary organizations pale in comparison to what is needed to do the job (Cooper, p.147).

However, to conclude that minimal is nonessential

would be very mistaken. The flexibility that private or volunteer organizations have allows them to adapt their programs to meet the most critical and un-addressed needs that homeless people are unable to find solutions for elsewhere

---

Profile:
Grass Roots

Although many organizations have been involved with the homeless, two are often mentioned as outstanding models.

Habitat for Humanity helps poor people throughout the U.S. and the world build their own homes. Habitat provides materials and money to assist the self-help efforts of people who want to build or renovate simple but decent houses. Construction is a cooperative effort involving home recipients and volunteers. No-interest mortgages are repaid to Habitat over a 15 to 25 year period. House payments, typically fixed at about 30 percent of the new owner's income, are recycled to build more homes. New homeowners in San Diego pay about $250 a month for a 1000 square foot, two bedroom, one bath home.

Organized in 1976, Habitat now has about 250 projects in the United States and has built more than 2500 homes worldwide. Habitat relies on local groups to decide who will become recipients and accepts local standards and customs regarding construction or design. Former President Jimmy Carter has been a long-time Habitat volunteer.

The Enterprise Foundation was formed in 1982 by real estate developer James Rouse, who is probably better known for his creative urban redevelopment efforts in many cities around the country. While building his festival marketplaces that replaced slums, he often saw the worlds of the rich and poor collide and wondered if there was any way that private enterprise could change the great inequities. With initial experience from a project in Washington D.C. that revitalized 350 housing units, and as the chair of the congressionally created National Housing Task Force, Rouse became convinced that the federal government should stimulate local efforts to provide low-cost housing. Working through nonprofit, grass roots groups that serve the poor, the foundation provides technical assistance, small grants, and loans to help tie together public and private funds for low income housing rehabilitation. Enterprise has worked with more than 900 individuals, foundations, and corporations that have provided over $429 million to rehabilitate over 17,000 residences.

Foundation experts have investigated ways to reduce current housing rehabilitation costs, such as reducing room size, using alternative building materials, setting up nonprofit donated materials warehouses, and have experimented with newly constructed modular homes that have sold for less than $30,000 in suburban areas. Other foundation efforts are directed toward seeking out home financing alternatives, and helping to develop partnerships between public and private sectors.

Prospects for the future. Experts have often described a three-tier approach to homeless problems. This model is useful to help understand the various roles of local public and private agencies and the necessary role of the federal government to resolve the problems of homelessness. The three tiers include emergency, transitional, and long-term programs.

Emergency needs. Homeless people, whether labelled "deserving" or "nondeserving," or whether they are permanently or episodically in this condition, are all in need of emergency shelter or services at some time. As we know from earlier chapters, the actual number of homeless individuals is likely much larger than any official one-time count. And, if an unusual combination of events were to occur in a particular locale, the number could become even greater. Therefore, the problem that most cities have is in anticipating these needs and properly funding and coordinating them. Since the 1970s many cities have become familiar with the nature of the homeless problem and have learned how to provide emergency assistance.

Should additional money be spent on creating or improving shelters? Considering their rudimentary nature, it would be no surprise that additional money could be used for improvements. But should full-service shelters be phased out as soon as housing programs can provide adequate dwellings for unattached persons? Although they will probably always be needed, their limited privacy, security concerns, and physical environment rarely meet any common standards of minimally decent housing. Rossi feels that the "prospect of dormitory living for the unattached poor could become a fixed feature of our cities" either because of expediency or "shelter industry" interests (Rossi, p.203). Currently, many cities and states are debating whether to expand or even continue shelter funding and many hope to phase them out in the future. The most promising efforts have involved changing shelters into transitional housing, as discussed below. A related discussion sometimes heard among shelter providers concerns the proper role of a shelter. Some feel that the shelter's best efforts should be directed toward those individuals who demonstrate the greatest likelihood of future success. Other providers feel that a shelter's obligation is to serve all those in need.

Research indicates that many homeless people do not receive government benefits for which they qualify. Many do not receive Social Security disability payments, food stamps, AFDC payments or General Assistance, when available. This low participation indicates the difficulty that homeless people have in negotiating the welfare bureaucracy without some type of professional assistance. Model shelters, such as the recently opened 306-bed "megamission" in Los Angeles, now offer centralized and coordinated benefits counseling along with a variety of other services.

Some experts have recommended changes in policies for the homeless mentally ill. Although deinstitutionalization no longer is a major factor contributing to homelessness, a large number of recently released patients will likely experience homelessness within months. In addition, many more people who would have been admitted to mental hospitals in the past are not admitted today. In one view, mentally ill homeless are "protected" from obtaining medical help due to an extension of their rights. Others suggest that it would be better to hospitalize seriously impaired individuals who are rarely "protected" in the streets or shelters.

A variety of other suggestions have been made by both sociologists and other practitioners. For example, cities could develop or improve emergency food networks to support individuals and local feeding and shelter programs. Increasing public facilities, such as bathrooms or even portable toilets, would provide necessary services at convenient places. It is also still possible to learn from successful or existing programs and implement new ideas as they become proven.

Transitional phase. Homeless people suffer from a variety of maladies, conditions, and situations that often defy conventional solutions. Solving a housing problem is not sufficient if one is mentally ill or a substance abuser, or if jobs or benefits are only temporary. Often, people who are recently sheltered require a transitional period to stabilize their lives. Comprehensive programs must be available to provide a whole variety of services including job placement, job coaching, and counseling on a wide range of topics including substance abuse, nutrition, child care, and social benefits. Model programs offering the opportunity to drastically change one's life in a new setting may provide the vehicle for people to regain a productive life.

Sometimes, the transition to stabilization may be hampered by inability to find acceptable housing, even though funds are available. People may need help negotiating the complex search and qualification process at a time when other problems are being treated.

Advocacy and litigation may begin to focus more on transitional concerns now that many battles have been successfully waged to gain such basics as the right to emergency shelter, minimum shelter quality standards, and the removal of barriers to emergency assistance. For example, attempting to concentrate transitional programs and services in a new neighborhood would likely run into problems with local zoning policies and other "not in my backyard" objections. Greater advocacy of useful transitional ideas might demonstrate their value in the long run, or obligate communities to recognize the necessity of stabilization programs.

Long-term proposals. Despite much public attention, resolution of legal disputes, and the passage of significant legislation, there remain as many homeless or nearly homeless now as there were in the 1980s. Obviously many of the same basic conditions continue to exist that impede any long-term solution of the problem. Despite the general increase in emergency shelters and services, and the best efforts of existing rehabilitation and benefits programs, many homeless people will describe their experiences as not unlike a revolving door. Unfortunately, the

necessary solutions, which include permanent
suitable housing, regular sustainable employment
or adequate support, and health and related social
benefits, continue to be lacking. Experts
recommend a variety of specific long-term
proposals to successfully deal with today's
homelessness problem.

First of all, housing subsidies should be increased
to reflect the real costs of housing in cities. The
limited subsidies available today are less than
what is found in comparable industrial countries,
and do not provide adequate assistance to pay real
rental expenses. Alternatively, some have
suggested increasing rent control policies to limit
the effects that gentrification or economic
fluctuations may have upon rent. Whether the
regulatory effects of rent control impedes free-
market growth is often debated. Nevertheless,
there are long waiting periods for subsidized
housing, and the private housing market has
failed to meet the recent needs of single poor
people.

In addition, new housing needs to be built or
rehabilitated to fill the nation's general inventory
so that a greater proportion is available to all
types of poor people. Since construction of low-
income housing is almost never profitable, and
since housing construction has been dominated by
private industry, either subsidies to builders or
benefits to residents to help offset construction
costs must be continued and expanded.
Development of cooperatives with resale

restrictions to provide multifamily community-based housing through a nonprofit corporation could be encouraged. Many of the benefits of ownership can be obtained without depending upon the unpredictability of the private marketplace (Gilderbloom and Appelbaum, p.152). Similarly, the development of community "land trusts" offers promise. Today, over 120 nonprofit organizations in cities across the nation have purchased land to develop housing for rent or sale, while retaining title to the land. Since buyers are not paying for the land, costs of buying can be reduced by an estimated twenty-five percent (Ouellette, p.38). Other alternative approaches may also be continued, although many are no longer considered innovative. Some have suggested converting military barracks, building more prefab and manufactured housing, refining construction methods, and using alternative materials. However, these efforts, as visionary as they may be, are sometimes too costly, are located in places where no one wants to live, and may not be affordable to poor people unless subsidies are available. In addition, barriers to low-income housing proposals are often created in non poor areas which further limits the spaces that are deemed suitable for affordable housing. Patterns of residential segregation by race are still strong in many cities and evidence of active discrimination is clear. More concerted efforts by federal, state, and local governments are necessary to remedy the situation.

Employment patterns. The shift in the United

States from manufacturing to a service economy has been a major contributor to homelessness. Many cities have seen their job market change drastically in less than a decade with the result that the most vulnerable people at the bottom suddenly become homeless. These changes, when combined with a general economic slowdown, indicate a generally dismal employment future for people at the bottom. Unlike their parents, people who possess limited education and training today can no longer find jobs that will provide an income sufficient to support a family. Many experts have suggested that greater emphasis should be placed on public education to provide more sophisticated job training and apprenticeship programs and encourage employers to invest more in the continuous education and training of their workers (Burt, p.223). The development of regional job-training centers and an increase of national service programs may help to counter unemployment or other social problems that eventually lead to a high risk of becoming homeless. Unfortunately, many past job-training programs have been hampered by politics and thus experienced short program histories. As programs come and go, faith in their credibility by both potential employers and clients diminish. In addition, economic globalization is likely to limit this country's efforts to dramatically restructure employment opportunities or income potential in the near future. If this is true, then greater emphasis should instead be directed toward making housing more affordable.

Benefits. Research also shows that benefits have not matched inflation in the last decade. In addition, there is an almost complete lack of program coverage for the type of people who make up most of the homeless population. For benefits to prevent homelessness, they must first reach vulnerable households and then provide enough to allow the recipient to pay the rent. Very few benefit programs do both, with the result that the largest homeless group, unattached males, receives the least (Burt, p.223).

These recommendations are not unknown to public officials or policymakers. Many have been recommended for years and others have been part of model programs in one or more locations. Why, then, have they not been adopted in a comprehensive manner? Much of the explanation for inaction must come from the cultural beliefs and attitudes of elected public officials. Perhaps there has been an even greater collection of deeply rooted ideas about success and failure, worthiness and ambition, and personalized fault that has had the net effect of preventing implementation of major policy changes that experts have suggested. In addition, the homeless are not an attractive group in a country where appearance counts. They suffer from a variety of maladies and many people find it difficult not to associate their condition with reprehensible personal qualities. Also, the homeless have usually been an outgroup during a governing era that has stressed acquisition and greed. Homeless people must wonder where the sensibilities of the nation have gone when they watch rich real estate investors supervise neighborhood "tear-downs"- the replacement of old homes with multimillion dollar palaces that feature private petting zoos and motorized chandeliers (Phillips, p.211).   Homeless people need advocates or supporters that will counter the interests of those who stand to gain from profit-oriented housing policies or development regulations.   Homeless people also need advocates to redirect funds to resolve their plight in a time of a massive federal deficit and occasionally dwindling state and local revenues.

Today, the cultural legacy of blame-the-victim thinking still persists. People continue to distinguish between the worthy and unworthy poor. Some still feel that homeless people chose their way of life and ought to rely on their own efforts to get out of that predicament. They continue to believe that homelessness is largely a personal problem that requires personal solutions. They believe that homeless people should be arrested, cured, or committed. If these erroneous perceptions continue to significantly influence public policy, and if politicians who pander to such attitudes are elected, then government will continue to ignore the needed changes. Instead, politicians need to stand for the greater American cultural traditions that stress equality of opportunity, the dignity of people, and the right to a decent life without a myriad of qualifications and exceptions. As public officials continue to be increasingly drawn from a wider range of progressive social, economic, and cultural groups,

the development of more empathetic attitudes
toward the homeless will increase.

Nevertheless, salutary and decent efforts do not go
without recognition. Countless endeavors by
officials and volunteers have touched the lives of
those who now have a home. Despite occasional
setbacks, optimism will continue to feed the cause
of those who know that the right solutions are not
out of place, but just inside the front door.

References

Abu-Lughod, Janet L. *Changing Cities: Urban Sociology*. New York: HarperCollins Publishers, 1991.

Adelson, Joseph. "The Ideology of Homelessness." *Commentary*, March, 1991, 32-36.

Bahr, Howard M. *Skid Row*. New York: Oxford University Press, 1973.

Banfield, Edward C. *The Unheavenly City Revisited*. Massachusetts: Little, Brown and Company, 1974.

Becker, Howard S. *Outsiders*. New York: Free Press, 1973.

Brinkley, David. *Washington Goes To War*. New York: Ballantine Books, 1988.

Burt, Martha R. *Over the Edge: The Growth of Homelessness in the* 1980s. New York: Russell Sage Foundation, 1990.

Caton, Carol L. M. "Homelessness in Historical Perspective." In *Homeless in America*, ed. Carol L. M. Caton, 3-18. New York: Oxford University Press, 1990.

Coates, Robert C. *A Street Is Not A Home*: *Solving America's Homeless Dilemma*. New York: Prometheus Books, 1990.

Cooper, Mary Anderson. "The Role of Religious and Nonprofit Organizations in Combating Homelessness." In *The Homeless in Contemporary Society*, ed. Richard D. Bingham, Roy E. Green and Sammis B. White, 130-149. California: Sage Publications, 1987.

Del Valle, Christina. "Low Income Housing: Is There a Better Way?" *Business Week*, June 22, 1992, 61-62.

DiIulio, John Jr., "There But For Fortune." *New Republic*, 24 June 1991, 27-36.

Doan, Michael. "Washington's Hero of the Homeless." *U.S. News and World Report*, June 16, 1986, 11

Dreier, Peter and Richard Appelbaum. "American Nightmare: Homelessness." *Challenge*, March/April, 1991, 46-52.

Dugger, Celia W. "Big Shelters Hold Terrors for the Mentally Ill." New York Times, January 12, 1992, 1,22

Encyclopedic Dictionary of Sociology. Connecticut: Dushkin Publishing Group, 1986.

Enterprise Foundation 1991 *Annual Report.*
Maryland: Enterprise Foundation.

Gans, Herbert J. *The Levittowners.* New York:
Vintage Books, 1967.

Gilderbloom, John I. and Richard P. Appelbaum.
"A National Housing Policy Would Help the
Homeless" in *The Homeless: Opposing Viewpoints,*
ed. Lisa Orr, 150-155. California: Greenhaven
Press, 1990.

Gorder, Cheryl. *Homeless! Without Address in
America.* Arizona: Blue Bird Publishing, 1988.

Guest, Edgar A. *Home.* in *A Treasury of the
Familiar.* Woods, Ralph L., ed., 79. New York: The
MacMillan Co., 1955

Harrison, Bennett, and Bary Bluestone. *The
Great U–Turn: Corporate Restructuring and the
Polarizing of America.* New York: Basic Books,
1988.

Harvey, F. Barton. "A New Enterprise."
Humanist, May/June, 1989, 14-15, 38.

Hess, Beth B. *Sociology.* 4th ed. New York:
Macmillan Publishing, 1991.

Hopper, Kim. "Advocacy for the Homeless in the
1980s." in *Homeless in America*, ed. Carol L. M.
Caton, 160-173. New York: Oxford University
Press, 1990.

Hope, Marjorie. *The Faces of Homelessness*. Massachusetts: Lexington Books, 1986.

Jackson, Michele. "The McKinney Bill." *Nation's Cities Weekly*, January 2, 1989, 3

Kaufman, Nancy K. "Homelessness: A Comprehensive Policy Approach" in *Housing the Homeless*, ed. Jon Erickson, 335-345. New Jersey: Center for Urban Policy Research, 1986.

King, Charles E. "Homelessness in America." *Humanist*, May/June, 1989, 8,32.

Kozol, Jonathan. *Rachel and Her Children*. New York: Crown Publishers, 1988.

Lenski, Gerhard Emmanuel. *Human Societies*. New York: McGraw-Hill, 1987.

Lewis, Oscar. *Four Families: Mexican Case Studies in the Culture of Poverty*. New York: Basic Books, 1959.

Lincoln Village: Protective Restrictions. County of San Joaquin, California, 1948.

McCarthy, Colman, "Mitch Snyder." *The Nation*, July 30/August 6, 1990, 116.

Minnish, Harvey C., ed. *Old Favorites from the McGuffey Readers*. New York: American Book Co., 1936

Mumford, Lewis. *The City in History*. New York: Harcourt, Brace and World, 1961.

Nathan, Richard P. "Institutional Change and the Challenge of the Underclass." *Annals of the American Academy of Political and Social Sciences*, January, 1989, 170-181.

New York Times. "Homeless by Choice? Some Choice", February 7, 1984, A24.

Novotny, Ann. *Strangers At The Door*. Connecticut: Chatham Press, 1971.

"Off the Street and Out of the Cold." *Time*, February 8, 1982, 66.

Ouellette, Laurie. "Land Trusts: An Answer to the Housing Crisis." *Utne Reader*, July/August, 1991, 38-40.

Palen, J. John. *The Urban World*. New York: McGraw-Hill, 1987.

Phillips, Kevin. *The Politics of Rich and Poor*. New York: HarperCollins Publishers, 1990.

Rael, Issac. *Madness in the Streets*. New York: The Free Press, 1991.

Raines, John C. *Illusions of Success*. Pennsylvania: Judson Press, 1975.

Robertson, Ian. *Sociology*. 3rd ed. New York: Worth Publishing, 1987.

Ropers, Richard H. *The Invisible Homeless: A New Urban Ecology*. New York: Human Services Press, 1988.

Ropers, Richard H. *Persistent Poverty: The American Dream Turned Nightmare*. New York: Plenum Press, 1991.

Rossi, Peter H. *Down and Out in America: The Origins of Homelessness*. Chicago: University of Chicago Press, 1989.

Rossi, Peter H. and James D. Wright. "The Urban Homeless: A Portrait of Urban Dislocation." *Annals of the American Academy of Political and Social Sciences*. January, 1989, 132-142.

Sanjek, Roger. "Federal Housing Programs and Their Impact on Homelessness" in *Housing the Homeless*, ed. Jon Erickson, 315-321. New Jersey: Center for Urban Policy Research, 1986.

Schneider, John C. "Skid Row as an Urban Neighborhood, 1800-1960" in *Housing the Homeless*, ed. Jon Erickson, 167-189. New Jersey: Center for Urban Policy Research, 1986.

Spates, James L. *The Sociology of Cities*. 2d ed. California: Wadsworth, 1987.

Spencer, Herbert. *Social Statics*. New York: D. Appleton and Co., 1880.

Spradley, James P. *You Owe Yourself a Drunk*. Massachusetts: Little, Brown and Company, 1970.

Talbot, Mary. "New York: The Wind Will Rattle Your Bones." *Newsweek*, December 2, 1991, 28.

Torrey, E. Fuller. "Who Goes Homeless?" *National Review*, 26 August, 1991, 34-36.

Tucker, William. "The Economies of Public Housing." *The American Spectator*, November 1989, 26-29.

Ward, David. *Poverty, Ethnicity, and the American City*, 1840–1925: *Changing Conceptions of the Slum and the Ghetto*. New York: Cambridge University Press, 1989.

Weitzman, Lenore J. *The Divorce Revolution: The Unexpected Social and Economic Consequences for Women and Children in America*. New York: Free Press, 1985.

Wilson, William Julius. *The Truly Disadvantaged*. Chicago: University of Chicago Press, 1987.

Wilson, William Julius. "The Underclass: Issues, Perspectives, and Public Policy." *Annals of the American Academy of Political and Social Sciences*. January, 1989, 182-192.

Wright, James D. "The Worthy and Unworthy
Homelessness." *Society*, July/August, 1988, 64-69.

Wright, James D. "Address unknown:
Homelessness in Contemporary America." *Society*,
September/October, 1989, 45-53.

Wright, John W. *The Universal Almanac*.
Missouri: Andrews and McMeel, 1992.